1/96

X

GENETICS

HUMAN

HEALTH

GENETICS & HUMAN HEALTH

A JOURNEY WITHIN

FAITH HICKMAN BRYNIE

Illustrated by Sharon Lane Holm

The Millbrook Press
Brookfield, Connecticut

Library of Congress Cataloging-in-Publication Data
Brynie, Faith Hickman, 1946–
Genetics and human health : a journey within / by Faith Hickman
Brynie.
p.   cm.
Includes bibliographical references and index.
Summary: In examining the role that genetics plays
in human health, this book introduces the essentials
of genetics and looks at the ways in which scientists
are attempting to correct genetic disorders.
ISBN 1-56294-545-9
1. Medical genetics—Juvenile literature.   2. Human genetics—
Juvenile literature.   [1. Genetics.   2. Medical genetics.]
I. Title.
RB155.B79   1995
616'.042—dc20   94-25832   CIP   AC

Photographs courtesy of UPI/Bettmann: p. 16;
Photo Researchers: pp. 24, 25, 32, 49, 62,
69, 72, 74; Cold Spring Harbor Laboratory
Archives: p. 59; Wide World: p. 79; Sam
Ogden: p. 83. Chart on p. 107 © Susan Offner.

Published by The Millbrook Press
2 Old New Milford Road
Brookfield, Connecticut 06804

Dedicated to Mom and Ann,
my closest ripples
in the gene pool.

*The author gratefully acknowledges
the expert critical reviews provided by
Dr. Ronald Davidson,
McMaster University
Medical Center (retired),
Hamilton, Ontario, Canada,*

and

*Dr. Ian Boussy,
Department of Biology,
Loyola University, Chicago.*

CONTENTS

INTRODUCTION

A Journey Within

13

CHAPTER ONE

Blueprint for Life

15

CHAPTER TWO

Father Gregor and His Garden

30

CHAPTER THREE

Enemies Within

45

CHAPTER FOUR

Tinkering with Tinkertoys

58

CHAPTER FIVE

The Gene Stalkers

77

CHAPTER SIX

The Gene Doctors

95

CONCLUSION

Memories of Your Journey

109

Notes 111
Glossary 115
Further Information 120
Index 124

GENETICS

HUMAN

HEALTH

A Journey Within

Come along on an incredible journey, a journey that will take you from a volleyball court in Los Angeles to a remote fishing village in Venezuela. You will travel across time as well, visiting a humble monk in the 1860s, some fun-loving model builders a century later, and scientists at work today.

The purpose of your journey will be to explore how traits inherited from parents, grandparents, and countless past generations affect the well-being of people now living. You will travel into the science of *genetics*, the study of inheritance, to see its effects on human health.

Crossing all barriers of space and size, you will enter the *cell*, the basic unit of life, to see how it works. You will tour factories inside the cell where the chemistry of life is engineered. There you will explore the cell's control center, the *nucleus*. You will unlock the mystery of the *gene*, the basic unit of inheritance, and discover the molecule *DNA*. DNA makes up the gene and directs everything the cell

13

does. DNA makes you human. It also makes you unique, different from every other person who has ever lived in the entire world.

You'll travel into the lives of some extraordinary people. You will meet an athlete who strove for Olympic gold, a small boy who has physical therapy every day of his life, a biologist who eventually won the Nobel Prize because he didn't want to learn chemistry, and a psychologist who faced a family tragedy by setting off to find a gene. Some have illnesses caused by DNA control systems gone wrong. Others spend their lives trying to help correct those systems and to stem their negative effects.

You will see why many genetic disorders can be predicted from family histories. You will investigate patterns of inheritance that all living things, from bacteria to pea plants to people, share. You will use some maps as you travel—not always complete or totally accurate maps, but good enough to guide you into the vast and expanding realm of genetics.

Finally, you are setting off on a journey within yourself. The more you learn about genetics and human health, the more you will face questions no scientist can answer. Should people be tested to learn if they carry a potentially harmful gene? If they are tested, who should know the results? How far should doctors go in their attempts to replace and repair genes? New genetic knowledge offers promise of great good, but can it also be turned to evil? Each of us must search for answers to these questions—not in laboratories, but in our minds, hearts, and consciences.

Are you ready to set off on your journey within? The secrets of life are awaiting you.

CHAPTER ONE

Blueprint for Life

"Flo Hyman can flat-out play," praised Ken Denlinger of the *Washington Post*. "She is 6 feet 5, skywalks on the same heavenly path as Michael Jordan and punches volleyballs as intensely as Joe Frazier ever nailed Ali."[1]

Tall, lanky Flo Hyman was the undisputed leader of the women's team they called the Great American Volleyball Machine. They were the superstars of the 1984 Summer Olympic Games in Los Angeles. Millions of Americans watched the championship match on television with high hopes. After all, the American women had defeated their opponents, the Chinese, in a previous round. "Anticipation was as giddy as any NCAA Final Four, Super Bowl or World Series I've seen," Denlinger wrote. "The American women dedicated their lives, some for as long as nine years, toward the once daffy notion of winning the Olympic gold medal."[2]

Sadly, the gold escaped them. Most of Flo Hyman's best spikes were blocked at the net or

U.S. volleyball player Flo Hyman (right) and
teammate Carolyn Becker with silver medals
won at the 1984 Olympic Games.

retrieved by the back-liners. China took the lead late in the first game and won the next two with ease. The Americans had to settle for the silver, but Flo was undaunted: "One must be first, one must be second. It all amounts to how well and determined you are, that day, to take it home. What I've done has been by choice. I feel fulfilled."[3]

Less than two years later, at age 31, Flo Hyman was dead.

During a professional volleyball match in Matsue, Japan, she suffered what appeared to be a heart attack. An autopsy showed that a tiny weak spot in her aorta, the large artery that carries blood away from the heart, had burst inside her chest. The weakness had been there since birth. No one had suspected that Flo Hyman had Marfan's syndrome, an inherited disorder.

INHERITED DISORDERS

An inherited disorder is a disease that passes from one person to another, but not in the way infectious diseases do. No virus or bacterium or other external agent causes an inherited disorder. Rather, the disorder is part of the person. It is a defect in the chemical instructions that tell cells what to do. Those instructions are carried in the egg cell and sperm cell that unite when a person is conceived. Flo Hyman had Marfan's syndrome because she inherited it from one of her parents.

About one person in 10,000 in the United States has Marfan's syndrome, for an estimated total of 30,000.[4] People with this inherited disorder are very tall and have very long fingers. Sometimes their breastbones are misshapen. They are usually nearsighted, and nearly all suffer the same weakness of the aorta that killed Flo Hyman. Some people think Abraham Lincoln—tall and lanky as he was—may have had Marfan's syndrome.

The symptoms of Marfan's arise from a defect in connective tissue, the support structure that holds the body together. Connective tissue forms the tendons that attach muscles to bones and the walls of blood vessels. Until recently, the reason for the weakness was unknown. The disease is inherited—that much was clear for a long time—but it wasn't until 1993 that scientists pinpointed the cause.

SYSTEMS, ORGANS, AND CELLS

To understand what happened to Flo Hyman and inherited disorders in general, consider some of the basic facts about how the human body is built. It is made up of systems, such as the circulatory system, skeletal system, and nervous system. Each system is a collection of organs working together. For example, the circulatory system comprises the heart, arteries, veins, and capillaries that pump and carry blood all around the body. Organs are made up of tissues. The heart consists of muscle tissue. Blood is a tissue too.

Tissues are built of cells, tiny structures usually too small to see without a microscope. Every tissue and organ is composed of millions of cells, each with its own unique structure and particular job to do. For example, muscle cells are different from bone cells, both of which are different from nerve, blood, and skin cells. These cells look different and do different jobs in the body, but they didn't start out different. Each cell came from the single cell that was the fertilized egg. The fertilized egg forms when a sperm cell from a man and an egg cell from a woman unite.

Shortly after fertilization, the egg divides into two cells, then four cells, then eight, then sixteen, and so on, until some 100 trillion cells make up a complete human body.[5] As organ systems start to form, various cells begin to look and act different, but deep inside, the vast majority are all the same. Nearly all cells carry the same set of instructions for making a human being. We call those instructions *genes*.

GENES

A gene is the blueprint for making some *molecule* (an assembly of atoms) that builds the living body or makes it work. For example, a gene tells the salivary glands in the mouth how to make a chemical, called amylase, that digests starch. That chemical kicks into action whenever a person eats potatoes or crackers. Another gene tells stomach cells how to make acid. That gene makes possible the digestion of meat, beans, and other protein foods. Still other genes tell the body how to make *hemoglobin*, the molecule that carries oxygen in the blood. Eyes and

19

hair are products of genes. Genes make eyes black, brown, hazel, or blue. They make hair straight or curly.

Genes account for other characteristics that run in families, such as right- or left-handedness, widow's peaks, straight or curved thumbs, cleft chins, and the presence or absence of hair on the fingers. A gene can also cause a disease such as Marfan's syndrome. The first clue that a disease may be inherited usually shows up in a *family tree*, a chart of relatives over several generations. Figure 1 is a chart of a family with Marfan's syndrome.

Family trees are easy to read. The generations are labeled with Roman numerals along the left-hand side. Individuals within each generation are numbered beginning with 1. Men are squares and women are circles. Married people without children and people who become parents are connected with a horizontal line. Their children are shown on a line below them and are connected to them with a vertical line. Thus, the great-grandparents I-1 and I-2 had four children, all girls. Only two of the girls married. Count the grandchildren of I-1 and I-2. There are five. Two of the grandchildren are married.

In the family tree, people who have died are shown with a slash. People having the characteristic of interest (in this case, Marfan's syndrome) have their circle or square colored in. In Figure 1, the boy and girl IV-1 and IV-2 have Marfan's syndrome. So does their mother, III-2, and their second cousins, III-5 and III-6. Their great-aunt II-5 also has the disorder.

Their grandmother, II-4, is dead, but we can guess that she probably had Marfan's syndrome too.

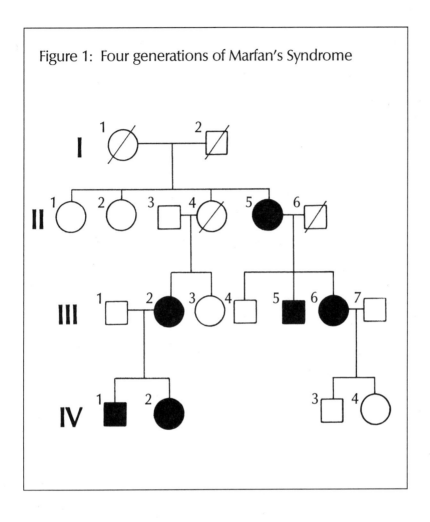

Figure 1: Four generations of Marfan's Syndrome

How do we know? Her children had it, and they must have received it from her since there is no history of the disease in her husband's family. Where did she get it? Either from her father or her mother, but we can't know which. The family tree doesn't tell us. One of them may have had Marfan's or, as happens in about a third of the cases, the gene may never have shown up in the family before.

That can happen because genes sometimes change for no apparent reason. (You'll learn how in Chapter Four.)

This family tree shows what scientists call a dominant pattern of inheritance. *Dominant* means that the characteristic shows up in every generation if families are large enough. Both males and females are affected. Only one parent is needed to pass the characteristic on to the next generation. There are exceptions, but most of the time the gene cannot hide. It passes from parent to child, and its effects show in every individual who receives it.

Seeing how genes pass from one generation to the next is only part of understanding how genes affect human well-being. You may still be wondering exactly what a gene is and how genes can determine why some children get a disorder like Marfan's and some don't. The answer lies in the architecture of the cell.

CELLS AND CHROMOSOMES

Figure 2 shows some parts of the cell. Notice the *cell membrane*. The membrane is important because it holds the cell together. It also determines which chemicals can enter and leave the cell. Inside the cell is the *cytoplasm*, the jellylike matter that forms most of the cell. Floating in the cytoplasm are two important kinds of structures—*mitochondria* and *ribosomes*. We will look at what they do in later chapters.

The core of the cell, the *nucleus*, is the dense region surrounded by its own membrane. Decades

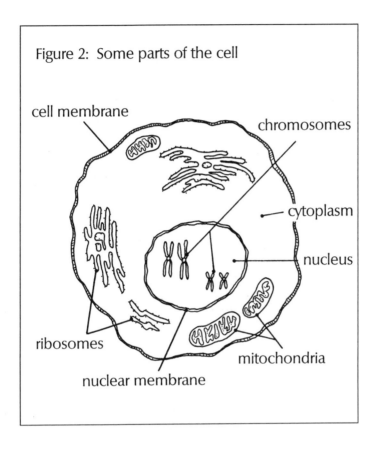

Figure 2: Some parts of the cell

cell membrane

chromosomes

cytoplasm

nucleus

ribosomes

mitochondria

nuclear membrane

ago, scientists found that cells cannot survive without a nucleus. (Red blood cells, which have no nucleus, are an exception.) The nucleus is the control center for the cell, providing all the instructions cells rely on to grow, develop, and reproduce. The genes, which carry these instructions, are located in the nucleus, lined up in orderly rows in structures called *chromosomes*.

In a normal human body cell, there are 46 chromosomes. The chromosomes are visible when cells divide. Cells can be stained and photographed

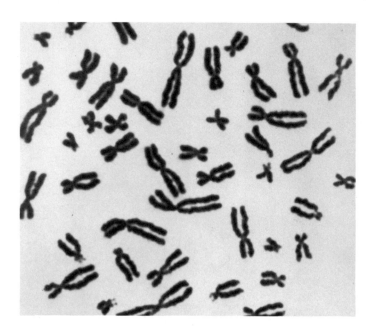

Chromosomes in the nucleus of a human cell.

through a microscope to show chromosomes. If the chromosomes in the photograph are cut out and arranged by size and shape, a pattern emerges. The chromosomes are in pairs, two of each kind, for a total of 23 pairs in females. Males have 22 pairs alike and one unmatched pair. The last pair are the sex chromosomes.

Scientists estimate that more than 100,000 genes work in the human body.[6] Think of the chromosomes as 46 strings of beads, each containing a few thousand beads. Think of the beads as genes. When everything is working right, half the chromosomes in a cell come from the mother and the other half come from the father. Each gene, then,

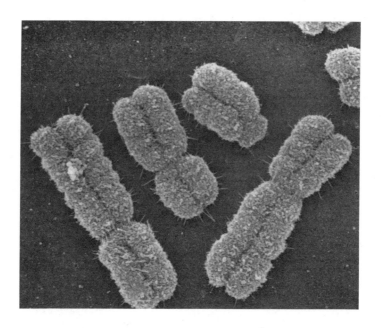

Human chromosomes magnified about 8,400 times.

has a duplicate on its matching chromosome. Chromosomes come in pairs. Genes come in pairs. Body cells get a double dose of each gene, but often only one gene in the pair does any work. The other gets "turned off." Switching off happens, too, when cells take on different shapes and functions. In a muscle cell, for example, the genes that make nerve cells, blood cells, and many other kinds of cells turn off. The genes that make muscle cells are the ones left operating.

An arithmetic problem arises here. Body cells have 46 chromosomes in 23 pairs, a double dose of each gene. If body cells served as sperm and egg, the next generation would get a double dose again.

There would be four of each gene instead of two; then the next generation would get eight and so on. Such doubling does not occur; no one would survive if it did. Even a few extra genes usually cause serious mental and physical abnormalities. For example, an extra chromosome 21 is the most common cause of Down's syndrome, a disorder characterized by heart abnormalities and mental retardation.

The answer to this arithmetic problem lies in how egg cells and sperm cells are made. When cells divide to make the reproductive cells, the chromosome pairs separate into different cells through a series of steps. Half the chromosomes end up in each reproductive cell. Each sperm cell or egg cell contains 23 chromosomes, one from each pair. When the egg is fertilized, 23 chromosomes from the mother pair up with 23 from the father, and the number is right again.

What does this have to do with Marfan's syndrome? Look again at the family tree in Figure 1 and consider the man III-5. He has Marfan's syndrome. So does his sister (III-6). They got it from their mother (II-5), but his brother (III-4) escaped the disease. Why? Because chromosome pairs separated when the mother's egg cells formed. On one of her chromosomes was the gene that makes connective tissue weak. On the other chromosome was a normal gene. When her egg cells formed, half got the Marfan's gene, half got the normal gene. Two of her three children received the gene by sheer chance, like the chance of flipping a coin and getting two heads and a tail in three tries.

Figure 3: Chromosomes arranged in pairs

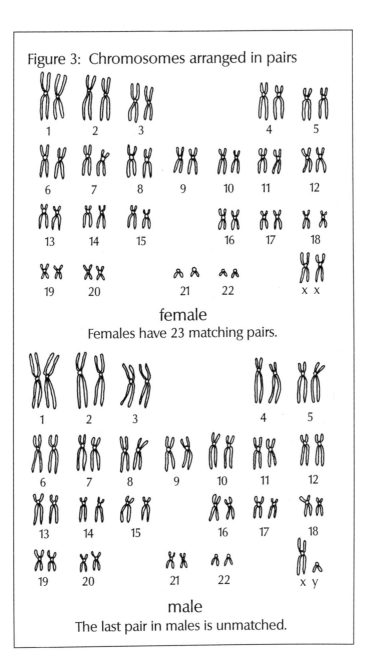

female

Females have 23 matching pairs.

male

The last pair in males is unmatched.

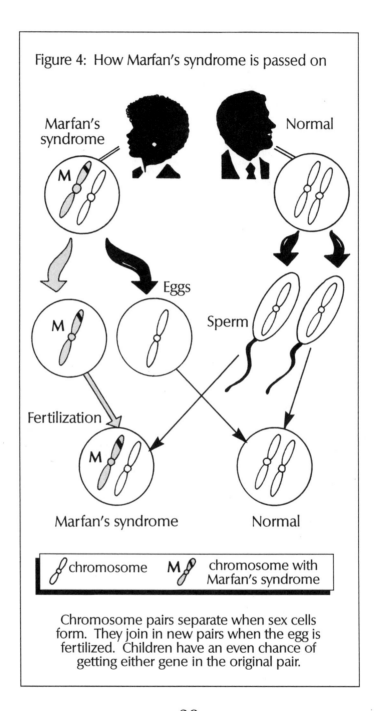

Figure 4: How Marfan's syndrome is passed on

Marfan's syndrome

Normal

Eggs

Sperm

Fertilization

Marfan's syndrome

Normal

chromosome   M   chromosome with
                              Marfan's syndrome

Chromosome pairs separate when sex cells
form. They join in new pairs when the egg is
fertilized. Children have an even chance of
getting either gene in the original pair.

The chance of passing Marfan's along to a child is one half, or 50-50. That's because half the egg or sperm cells get the faulty gene, and the gene always shows its effects in the child. Not all genes behave this way. Some don't show their effects until both genes in the pair are abnormal.

As important as inheritance is, there may be bigger lessons to learn from the story of Flo Hyman and the Great American Volleyball Machine. In a life cut tragically short, she did more than her share not only to bring the United States within striking distance of an Olympic gold, but also to promote women's sports in America. Flo Hyman was a model of dedication and good sportsmanship. In her honor, Major League Volleyball gives the Flo Hyman Award to the female athlete who "embodies the spirit and dignity" of the great volleyball star.[7] Martina Navratilova, Jackie Joyner-Kersee, and Chris Evert were among the first recipients of that honor.

CHAPTER TWO

Father Gregor and His Garden

How do we know what cells do? Who first described the patterns of heredity that make people so different from one another, yet alike in so many ways? To answer these and other questions we must leave the Olympic sports arena and travel to eastern Europe in the nineteenth century. There we will meet Gregor Mendel, an Augustinian monk, who planted peas along his monastery wall and watched them grow. Perhaps even he could not have guessed that his garden patch would reveal the secrets of life itself.

POOR MAN'S SON

The future monk was born and named Johann Mendel on July 22, 1822, in the village of Hyncice in what was then part of Austria but today lies within the Czech Republic. His father was a peasant farmer who was obliged to work for the lord of the manor without pay. The boy grew short, broad-shouldered, and sturdy. He shared his father's passion for growing fruit trees and was good at farmwork. He also did well in school, where reading and writing shared a place in the curriculum with fruit growing and beekeeping.

By age 11, Johann had outgrown the village school. He begged his father to send him to the school at Lipnik and a year later to the high school at Opava. Johann's father agreed, reluctantly giving up his dream that his son would take over his farm.

His parents had little money and were hard pressed to pay his school fees. Mendel survived through high school on half rations and must have endured more than a few pangs of hunger, despite the baskets of bread and butter his parents sent him. Although an illness had forced him to drop out of school for a while, he received his diploma at Opava in 1840 and set his sights on higher education at Olomouc University.

Financial problems worsened. In the winter of 1838, a rolling tree trunk crushed his father's chest. The elder Mendel could no longer do farmwork. The only choice was to sell the farm. The sale provided a pitifully small income for the young Mendel. Although he did well at Olomouc, poor health again forced his withdrawal in 1841.

An unselfish gift from Mendel's younger sister, Theresia, allowed him to return to school. She gave him her share of the money from the sale of the farm. Mendel studied the required subjects: religion, philosophy, math, Latin literature, and

Gregor Mendel laid the foundation for modern
genetic science, but his work was not appreciated
until after his death in 1884.

physics. The study of natural history—which today is considered part of biology and essential
background for a career in genetics—was denied
Mendel. He couldn't afford to pay the extra fees.

The gift from Mendel's sister didn't go far.
Again, facing money problems, he approached his
physics professor, Friedrich Franz, for help. A combination of luck, circumstance, and Mendel's excel-
lent record as a student saved the day. While

teaching at Brno, Franz had lived in the Augustinian monastery of St. Thomas and had made many friends there. They had asked him to recommend his best pupils to join the order. He suggested Mendel. At the age of twenty-one, Mendel took his vows as a novice and accepted his monastic name, Gregor, the name he used for the rest of his life.

Joining the monastery gave Mendel more than a guaranteed roof over his head and food on the table. Hugo Iltis, Mendel's biographer, described the monastery as "a place puls[ing] with artistic and scientific energy . . . one of the chief centres of the spiritual and intellectual life of the country."[1]

Mendel thrived in his new home. He studied the classics, as all novices did. In his spare time, he examined the rock and plant collections available at the monastery. Other monks who shared his interest in botany encouraged him.

In 1848, Mendel became a parish priest, a vocation that suited him not at all. A German-speaking Austrian, he struggled with the Czech language required for sermons to his Czech parishioners. Worse, he found the duty of attending the sick and dying intolerable, so much so that he became ill himself. Was it possible that Mendel was a hypochondriac? Maybe, but he was saved from his illnesses by another stroke of good fortune. His friend Prelate Napp, who was director of higher education for the region, appointed Father Gregor to a temporary job teaching at Znojmo High School.

Mendel was liked and respected by his students, but regulations said he could not hold a permanent position until he passed his teacher's exam. In 1850, Mendel took the exam. He failed, but landed another teaching job at the Brno Technical School—again on a temporary basis.

In 1854, he took another teaching position, this time at the Brno Modern School. He tried the teacher's exam again in 1856 and failed again. Someone must have pulled some strings for him somewhere, for Mendel continued to teach until 1868 without ever passing his exam. Mendel was happy as a teacher. By all accounts, he loved teaching and his pupils loved him. These were the years of his experiments with peas that earned him, long after his death, the unchallenged title Father of Genetics.

EXPERIMENTS WITH PEAS

Mendel chose peas for his experiments because they have easily observed characteristics and nearly all the seeds germinate when planted. Also, peas self-pollinate. That means a single plant can fertilize itself. How does that happen? *Stamens* are the male parts of a flower. They produce pollen, which contains the sperm cells. The female part of the plant is the *pistil* and contains egg cells at its base. The transfer of pollen to the pistil results in *fertilization*, the union of egg and sperm that must occur before seeds can form. Seeds form at the base of the pistil. The stamens of the pea usually release pollen before the flower is fully open, so the pistil of the plant is dusted with its own pollen early on, making chance fertilization by wind or insects unlikely. This characteristic meant that Mendel could control the parents: By removing the stamens, he could

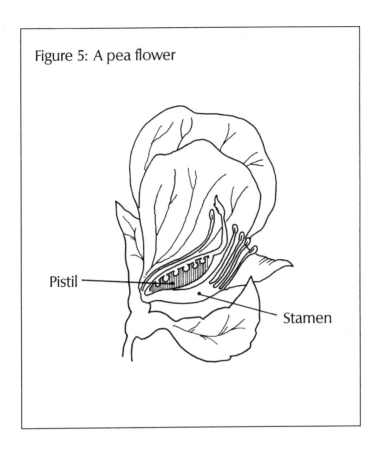

Figure 5: A pea flower

Pistil

Stamen

prevent self-pollination and fertilize the pistil with pollen from any male parent flower he chose.

First, Mendel tested varieties of peas until he was sure he'd found several that "bred true" for each of seven pairs of characteristics he decided to study. For example, he grew plants that always produced round seeds generation after generation. He grew others that always produced wrinkled seeds. Some plants always grew tall; others were always dwarf. Some produced only green pods. Others produced only yellow pods. These pairs of "true-breeding"

MENDEL'S EXPERIMENTS WITH PEAS

#	Pair of Characteristics	Total Plants	Total Seeds	Dominants (D)	Recessives (R)	Ratio (D:R)
1	Round seeds(D) Wrinkled seeds (R)		7,324	5,474	1,850	2.96 : 1
2	Yellow seed leaves (D) Green seed leaves (R)		8,023	6,022	2,001	3.01 : 1
3	Colored seed coat (D) White seed coat (R)	929		705	224	3.15 : 1
4	Inflated pod (D) Constricted pod (R)	1,181		882	299	2.95 : 1
5	Green pod (D) Yellow pod (R)	580		428	152	2.82 : 1
6	Side flower (D) End flower (R)	858		651	207	3.14 : 1
7	Tall stem (D) Dwarf stem (R)	1,064		787	277	2.84 : 1

plants Mendel chose as his parents for the next generation.

Mendel observed one pair of characteristics at a time. When he mated a green-pod plant with a yellow-pod plant, all the pods produced by the next generation were green. The characteristic that showed up in this first generation Mendel called *dominant*. For pod color, green was dominant. What had happened to the yellow pods, which Mendel called *recessive*? Were yellow pods lost forever?

To find out, Mendel allowed the first-generation green-pod plants to pollinate themselves. Then he observed the plants that grew from the next generation of seeds. He counted about three green-pod plants for every one yellow-pod plant. Yellow pods were not lost. They showed up in the next generation.

For all seven characteristics, he found the same pattern. One characteristic would disappear in the first generation, only to reappear in the second, and always in very nearly a three-to-one ratio.

DOMINANT AND RECESSIVE FACTORS

Mendel was a good mathematician. He realized that his observations could be explained if a characteristic were determined by "factors" that occur in pairs. (He never used the word *gene*.) Mendel suggested that factors could unite in the offspring of two true-breeding parents without being changed or lost. He wrote that the factors "only succeed in liberating themselves from the enforced tie of combination during the development of reproductive cells."[2] Mendel had deduced the behavior of chromosomes without ever seeing them.

Mendel explained his idea by using a capital letter to stand for a dominant factor, a small letter to represent a recessive factor. True-breeding green-pod plants have two identical dominant factors called G and G. True-breeding yellow-pod plants have two identical recessive factors g and g. Mendel realized that reproductive cells—sperm and egg—must carry only one half of the hereditary factors, thus giving the right number of factors again once sperm and egg unite. (If that were not true, hereditary material would double every generation, and that did not seem very likely.)

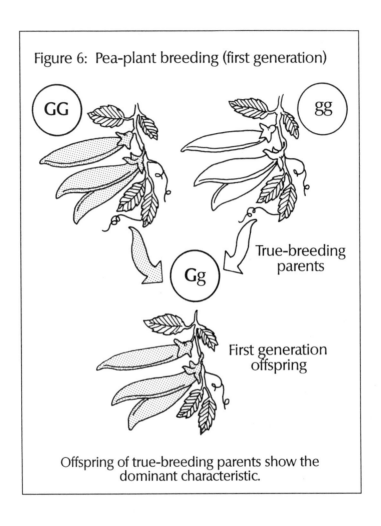

Figure 6: Pea-plant breeding (first generation)

GG

gg

Gg

True-breeding
parents

First generation
offspring

Offspring of true-breeding parents show the
dominant characteristic.

Since the true-breeding green-pod plant contains only the G factor, all its reproductive cells
must carry the G factor. In the same way, all the
reproductive cells of the yellow-pod plant carry
the g factor. Thus, the offspring of these two parents must all have the Gg combination of factors.
Since the dominant G is present in all, all have
green pods.

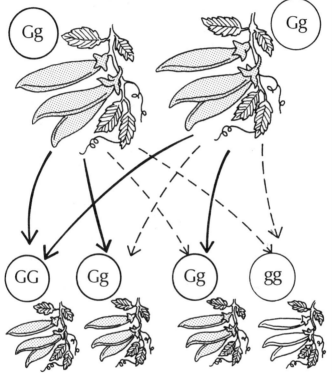

Figure 7: Pea-plant breeding (second generation)

First generation
offspring become parents

Gg

Gg

GG

Gg

Gg

gg

Offspring of plants with mixed hereditary
factors show dominant and recessive traits in a
three-to-one ratio.

But what happens in the next generation when Gg plants self-pollinate? Figure 7 shows the result. One half of the reproductive cells carry the G. The other half carry the g. When sperm and egg unite, one fourth of the offspring get two Gs, one from each parent. They have green pods, as do the half that have the Gg combination. But the final one fourth inherit a recessive factor from each parent. They have the gg combination. They have yellow pods because no dominant factor is present. This gives precisely the three-to-one ratio Mendel observed in his peas.

Mendel's work showed that inherited factors somehow stayed separate and distinct, despite the union of sperm and egg. Also, his results showed that characteristics are inherited independently; that is, one does not influence another. (We know today that's not always true. Mendel got lucky in the characteristics he observed. By chance, he selected seven characteristics carried on seven different chromosomes.) Mendel found that he could study pod color and height in the same plants, for example, and see each trait inherited independently of the other in that same three-to-one ratio.

SCIENCE LOST AND FORGOTTEN

In 1865, Mendel presented his findings to the Brno Society for the Study of Natural Science, which he had helped establish three years before. His work caused not a ripple in the scientific community.

Those few who read his paper either failed to understand it or failed to grasp its importance. Mendel, perhaps discouraged by the lack of response his work received, did no more work on inheritance, although he continued his plant-growing and weather experiments for many years.

Official duties further conspired to keep Mendel out of his garden. In 1868, he was elected prelate of the St. Thomas monastery. He was forced to resign his beloved teaching job. He became supervisor of the monastery estate, deputy of a mortgage bank, curator of the Institute for Deaf Mutes, and a key player in a decades-long dispute with the government over the taxation of monasteries. Mendel wrote his friends about how sad he felt neglecting his plants and bees.

Mendel suffered kidney disease for many years, made worse perhaps by his habit of smoking as many as 20 cigars a day, a practice he took up in a misguided attempt to battle his lifelong weight problem. Mendel died in 1884. Tragically, his journals were burned after his death, including most of his original handwritten notes on his pea experiments.

What survived was the modest paper "Experiments in Plant Hybridization," published in the proceedings of the little-known Brno Society. The principles he had found lay lost, forgotten, and unappreciated until 1900, when three independent researchers discovered his work and confirmed his findings through experiments of their own.

Scientists have now found a number of exceptions to the patterns Mendel uncovered. Still, what's remarkable about Father Gregor's work is not how little it explains, but how much. Inheritance follows Mendel's rules much of the time.

INHERITANCE AND DISEASE

Marfan's syndrome and many other inherited conditions that cause illness follow a dominant pattern of inheritance just as Mendel described it. To see how the pattern works, use a capital M to represent the gene for Marfan's syndrome and a small-letter m for the normal gene.

Now consider two parents, one who has Marfan's and one who does not. Remember, there are two genes for every characteristic. The parent with Marfan's probably has the Mm gene combination (since getting the gene from both parents is extremely unlikely). The normal parent has the mm combination, meaning two normal genes. What are the possibilities? The parent with Marfan's can make two kinds of reproductive cells. One kind— half the cells—will contain the M gene. The other half will contain the m gene. The normal parent can make only one kind of sex cell. All will contain the m gene. What happens when these genes pair up after the egg is fertilized? As you already know, each child has a 50-50 chance of getting the M gene and having Marfan's syndrome.

Mendel's laws apply far more widely than to pea plants. Scientists have found evidence of dominant and recessive inheritance in *organisms* (living things) ranging from the simplest bacteria to the

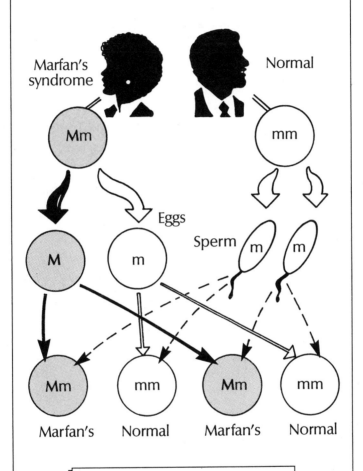

Figure 8: Inheritance of Marfan's syndrome

Marfan's syndrome

Normal

Mm

mm

Eggs

M   **m**

Sperm   m   m

Mm   **mm**   **Mm**   **mm**

Marfan's   Normal   Marfan's   Normal

M = Marfan's gene   m = Normal gene

The gene for Marfan's syndrome is dominant.
Each child has a one-in-two chance of having
the syndrome.

most complex animals, including human beings. Long before anyone had any idea of what a gene actually was, patterns of inheritance had been determined for many hundreds of genetic disorders. Today, over 3,500 genetic diseases are known, of which Marfan's is only one. Many do not follow the dominant pattern of inheritance, but they obey Mendel's laws nonetheless.

Let's journey next into the life of another individual who, as Flo Hyman did, suffers from a genetic disorder, and further examine patterns of inheritance.

CHAPTER THREE

Enemies Within

His parents named him Robert, but everyone calls him Bobby. He's as keen on baseball and as sour on girls as any other nine-year-old boy in his school. He likes science, hates spelling, and collects *Spider-man* comics. He is not allowed to have a dog, so he keeps an aquarium full of tropical fish. Bobby wants to be a sports reporter when he grows up. If he grows up.

What makes Bobby's future uncertain is not an outside threat. Bobby fears an enemy within himself—a disease called cystic fibrosis, or CF. CF isn't catching, but, as with many inherited diseases, parents can transmit it to their children without ever knowing it. That's what happened to Bobby. From his two perfectly healthy parents, he got the genes for cystic fibrosis. No one knew CF was there or saw it coming, and no one is to blame. But the enemy is real just the same.

CF is the most common genetic disease among white people. In the United States, about one in

45

every 2,000 children of Caucasian parents is born with the disease.[1] Few CF victims survive beyond the age of 30. Most die of lung infections.

CF produces in the lungs and digestive systems of its victims a thick, sticky mucus that interferes with both breathing and digestion. The mucus clogs the lungs, making them susceptible to infections. It also blocks digestion, so that people with CF have trouble getting adequate nourishment.

Bobby's day includes school, sports, friends, and family, just like all the other kids, but for Bobby there is a difference. His mom and dad take turns giving him one or two hours of physical therapy every morning and evening. They clap his chest and back and vibrate his body to loosen the mucus. Bobby coughs up as much as he can. Bobby often has to take antibiotics to fight lung infections. He also has to take pills called enzyme replacements. These provide extra doses of the chemicals that digest food. He also takes vitamins and nutritional supplements, sometimes as many as 40 pills a day. The pills don't always work. Bobby went into the hospital twice last year. The bill came to more than $10,000.

RECESSIVE DISORDERS

Neither of Bobby's parents ever heard of the disease in either of their families, although the gene is fairly common. About one in every 20 white Americans has the gene on one of his or her chromosomes.[2] But carrying the gene is not the same as having the

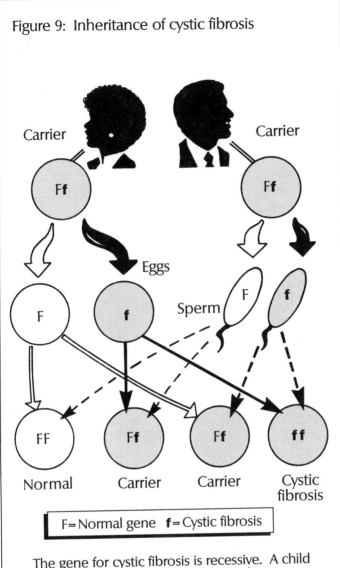

Figure 9: Inheritance of cystic fibrosis

Carrier

Carrier

Ff

Ff

Eggs

F

f

Sperm

F

f

FF

Ff

Ff

ff

Normal

Carrier

Carrier

Cystic
fibrosis

F = Normal gene   f = Cystic fibrosis

The gene for cystic fibrosis is recessive. A child
of parents who both carry the gene has a one-
in-four chance of having the disorder and a
one-in-two chance of being a carrier.

47

disease. It takes *two* CF genes, one from each parent, to make a child sick with CF. Because two genes are needed for the disease to show up, CF is called *recessive*. (Sometimes a single copy of a recessive gene is enough to cause a disease. That's called sex-linked inheritance, a special case we'll look at later.)

A person who receives a CF gene from one parent is normal. There are no signs of the disease. Such a person is called a *carrier*. Only when two carriers have a child can the disease appear. Recall how chromosome pairs separate when reproductive cells form. Pairs form again when the egg unites with a sperm cell. That process gives two carriers a one in four, or 25 percent, chance of having a child with cystic fibrosis.

Another recessive disorder is sickle-cell anemia. About 8 percent of American blacks carry the gene.[3] That means about one in every 600 babies of black parents is at risk for the disease.

Sickle-cell anemia arises from the inability of the body to make normal hemoglobin. *Hemoglobin* is the substance that carries oxygen in the blood. All the cells of the body need oxygen to stay alive. So oxygen must travel from the lungs to all the cells in the body to keep them alive. Victims of sickle-cell anemia make an abnormal hemoglobin. Like everyone else, the red cells in their blood contain hemoglobin and carry oxygen. Their red cells are shaped normally too, except when oxygen levels get low, as, for example, during exercise. Then the cells bend into a sickle shape. The sickle cells get tangled together and form jams of twisted cells. These jams sometimes block the tiny blood vessels that supply oxygen to all body tissues, interfering

48

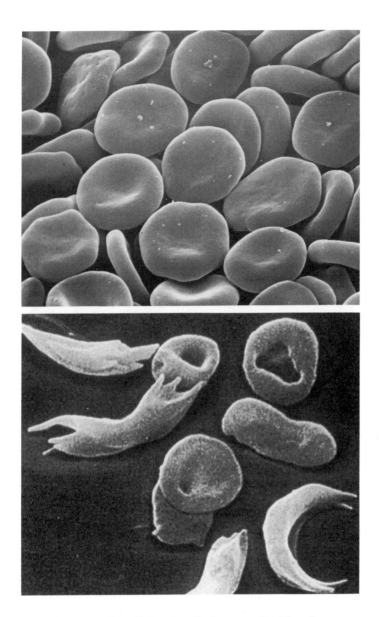

Top: Normal red blood cells have a disklike shape.
Bottom: In sickle-cell anemia, red blood cells are
distorted into crescents and other abnormal shapes.

with circulation and causing the death of cells starved of oxygen. If such jams occur in the heart or the brain, the person may die.

Sickle-cell anemia follows the same recessive pattern of inheritance as CF. The chance of two carriers having a child with sickle-cell anemia is one in four, or 25 percent.

One of the most tragic recessive disorders is Tay-Sachs disease. It appears most often in families of Eastern European (Ashkenazi) Jewish origin. Tay-Sachs babies grow and develop normally for the first few months of life. Then things start to change. The infant jerks just a little too much when it hears a loud noise. Next, a child that had already learned to smile, support its head, roll over, and sit up loses those skills. It goes into convulsions and becomes unaware of its environment. The head grows big, and vision is lost. Tay-Sachs children who live beyond the first year cease to move or communicate. Most die before they turn four. Tay-Sachs disease is incurable and always fatal.

The defect that causes Tay-Sachs has been known since 1962. A fatty substance called G_{M2} ganglioside builds up to excessively high levels in nerve cells. That happens because Tay-Sachs victims are missing the chemical that normally breaks down the fat. G_{M2} damages and destroys nerve cells, producing the symptoms of the disease.

Children with this deadly disorder are born to perfectly healthy parents. Carrier parents don't have Tay-Sachs because one of the genes in their gene pair is normal. It causes the cells to make enough of the chemical that breaks down the fat G_{M2} and keeps it from accumulating. It's only when no normal gene is present and no breakdown chemical is made that the trouble appears.

GENETIC DISORDERS AND ETHNIC ORIGINS

These examples—CF in whites, sickle cell in blacks, Tay-Sachs among Jews—show a pattern. Many genetic diseases turn up more frequently in certain ethnic groups. Pacific Islanders are at high risk for diabetes. People with ancestors from the Mediterranean region of Europe face a greater risk of a disease similar to sickle cell called beta-thalessemia. Why do genetic diseases concentrate in particular groups?

The answer requires a brief review of natural selection and evolution theory. The 19th-century naturalist Charles Darwin suggested that living things change over many generations because the "fittest" individuals are more likely to survive and reproduce than the less fit. To understand what Darwin meant, consider the cheetah's ability to run fast as an example. The cheetah is a predator that depends on its superior speed to overtake its prey. The fastest cheetahs are more likely to catch food than slower ones. The speedier cheetahs survive to reproductive age and pass along to their cubs the characteristics that make them swift. Slower cheetahs fail at hunting and starve before parenting litters. So, over thousands of years, cheetahs have evolved into the fastest land animal, able to run faster than 60 miles (100 kilometers) an hour.

Genes determine physical and chemical characteristics. Just as genes make cheetahs fast, they also cause genetic disease. But if a disease is life-threatening or fatal, how can the gene survive in the population? After all, before modern treatment, few CF or sickle-cell children survived long enough to become parents themselves, and Tay-Sachs victims still do not.

The first hint of an answer to this question came from observations in Africa. The sickle-cell gene was most common in those areas where malaria was also common. Could the gene somehow protect its carriers against malaria? It turned out that the answer is yes. While persons carrying two sickle-cell genes may sicken and die, those having one such gene have a built-in resistance to malaria. When the parasite that causes malaria infects their blood cells, the cells become sickle-shaped. These cells then die or are destroyed by the body, so the parasite never gets a chance to multiply in the person's bloodstream. As humans lived and evolved in Africa over many thousands of years, carrying one copy of the sickle-cell gene was an advantage to survival, so the gene flourished. American blacks no longer face much risk of malaria, but the gene is still there.

The same kind of idea may explain the frequency of Tay-Sachs among some groups of Jews. Several scientists have guessed that the Tay-Sachs gene, when present as one member of a gene pair, may make its carrier resistant to tuberculosis. All the facts aren't in and no one knows for sure, but the explanation is attractive. No one has yet ventured a guess about why CF is most common among whites.

There are other disorders that occur most frequently among other ethnic groups. In truth, no race or nationality is exempt. A vulnerability to genetic disease is shared by all human beings in every corner of the globe.

SEX-LINKED INHERITANCE

Before leaving the subject of genetic disease, let's look at two other patterns of inheritance. The first, called *sex-linked* inheritance, involves the chromosomes that determine sex. Recall that the last two chromosomes differ in males and females. Females have a matching pair, but males do not. These are the *sex chromosomes*. The larger one is called the X chromosome. The smaller is the Y. Usually, females have two X chromosomes. Most males have one X and one Y.

(Exceptions occur. Some females are XY, and some males are XX. Some females have a single X chromosome; some males have an X and two Y chromosomes. Other patterns such as XXY also occur rarely. This happens because something goes wrong when the mother's egg cell or the father's sperm cell is formed. One of the sex chromosomes gets lost or duplicated.)

The Y chromosome carries the instructions that cause an *embryo* (a higher organism early in its development) to become a male, but not very many other genes. The X chromosome carries many more genes that have nothing to do with sex, many that have no counterpart on the Y chromosome. So, for those characteristics, females get two genes, but males get only one.

Therefore, a recessive gene carried on the X chromosome is more likely to show its effects in a male than in a female. Females usually don't have the disorder because it is very unlikely that they'll get the gene from both parents. For that to happen, the mother would have to carry the gene and the father would have to have the disorder. One normal gene on one X chromosome is usually enough to keep things working normally. (There are a few dominant genes that cause disorders carried on the X chromosome. Their effects are usually milder in females than in males.)

A crippling disease called Duchenne's muscular dystrophy is inherited as a sex-linked recessive disorder. Victims start having trouble walking at about age four and are usually confined to a wheelchair by age 11. Death usually occurs in the later teens or twenties when breathing fails. People with this disease cannot produce a substance that protects muscle cells from damage during contraction. Without this substance, muscle cells slowly die.

The recessive gene for this type of muscular dystrophy is carried on the X chromosome. Women can carry the gene without ever knowing it until they give birth to a son with the disease. Their daughters have a 50-50 chance of being carriers.

Color blindness, with rare exceptions, is inherited according to the sex-linked pattern, as is hemophilia. Hemophilia, which usually affects only boys, can be a serious blood disorder. Victims lack adequate amounts of one or more of the chemicals that make blood clot. They suffer many bruises.

Figure 10: The inheritance of a sex-linked disorder

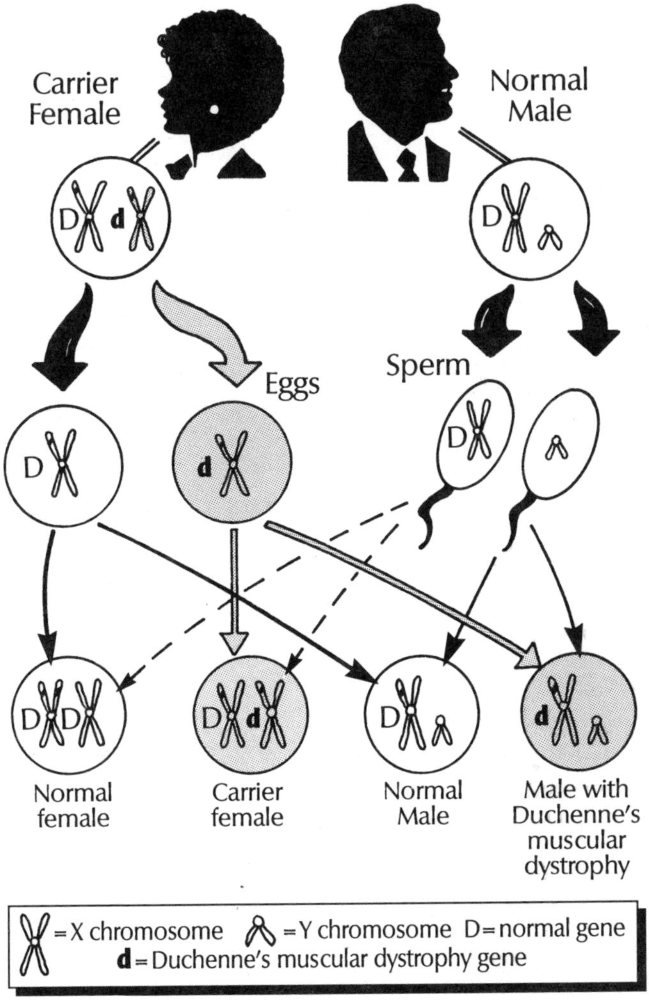
Carrier
Female
Normal
Male
D
d
D
Eggs
Sperm
D
d
D
D D
D d
D
d
Normal
female
Carrier
female
Normal
Male
Male with
Duchenne's
muscular
dystrophy
=X chromosome
=Y chromosome
D=normal gene
d=Duchenne's muscular dystrophy gene

The mother carries the gene for Duchenne's muscular dystrophy on her X chromosome. There are four possibilities among her children.

Cuts bleed for a long time. The slightest injury can cause internal bleeding, leading to painful swelling and accumulation of scar tissues in the joints. Today, good forms of treatment are available for boys with hemophilia. The factor missing from their blood can be injected. Still, threats from major injury are serious, and care must be taken before any surgery, even minor dental work.

As is so often the case with all genetic disorders, some individuals are more severely affected than others. Some people with hemophilia are hardly sick at all, and no one is quite sure why. Maybe the gene occurs in slightly different forms in different families. Perhaps the action of the gene is influenced by other genes. In any case, it's apparent that just as individuals vary, so also do the disorders they inherit.

MANY FACTORS, MANY GENES

The final form of inheritance is the one we see most and understand least. This is what scientists call *multifactorial* inheritance, meaning "many factors" are involved. Some of the factors are genes, probably several pairs of genes, so the genetic contribution is called *polygenic*. Height and blood pressure are polygenic characteristics. Many genes determine them. Environmental factors also get into the act. For example, nutrition affects height and stress can raise blood pressure. Multifactorial disorders arise when many genes interact with toxic factors in the physical or social environment. Some common multifactorial disorders include cleft lip and palate, schizophrenia, high blood pressure, diabetes, and many allergies. Even heart disease and cancer are at least partly multifactorial genetic disorders. Particular genes seem to make these diseases more or less likely in certain individuals.

These examples tell us something about how genes affect human health, but the fundamental question "What is the gene?" is still only partly answered. It took nearly a century after Mendel to unravel that mystery. To see how it was done, we must travel again through time and space to a laboratory in England where two grown men experimented with—of all things—Tinkertoys.

CHAPTER FOUR

Tinkering with Tinkertoys

"And so we had lunch, telling each other that a structure this pretty just had to exist. With the tension now off, I went to play tennis."[1] So recalled James Watson of the day he and Francis Crick finished the molecular model that was to earn them a Nobel Prize. The year was 1953. Watson and Crick had tinkered with cardboard cutouts and bits of wire and metal until they were sure they had it right. They'd built a model of DNA, the molecule that they believed was the gene.

The big celebration came forty years later. On March 5, 1993, 130 of science's top names gathered at Cold Spring Harbor Laboratory on New York's Long Island, to celebrate the birthday of a molecule. At the party, Watson, who was only 24 years old when he built the model, said, "The rest of my life has been spent trying to prove that I was almost equal to being associated with DNA." Crick said simply, "We were upstaged by a molecule."[2]

Watson and Crick with their DNA model.

RESTLESS YOUTH

Science writer Stephen Hall has described Watson as a "lanky, leering lad" with "restless, evasive eyes."[3] As a youth, Watson sought work on a wildlife refuge in the western United States. He ended up instead at the University of Indiana studying viruses that infect bacteria. Watson quickly grew bored and shifted his attention to genetics. He wrote in his book *The Double Helix*: "My interest in DNA had grown out of a desire, first picked up while a senior in college, to learn what the gene was."

Watson was asking a fundamental question that had remained unanswered since the term *gene* was coined in the early 1900s. The word was originally used to describe Mendel's "factors" or "particles"—those pieces of the cell that transmitted traits from parents to offspring. Trouble was, no one knew what those pieces actually were, although their association with chromosomes seemed obvious. By the 1940s, scientists accepted that genes must be some kind of protein found in the chromosomes. The first clue that they might be wrong came in 1944 from O. T. Avery's work at the Rockefeller Institute in New York. His experiments showed that traits could be transmitted from one cell to another by purified DNA molecules.

Watson saw DNA as a challenge and an opportunity, but his background left much to be desired. As he wrote:

> It was my hope that the gene might be solved without my learning any chemistry. This wish

partially arose from laziness since, as an under-graduate at the University of Chicago, I was prin-cipally interested in birds and managed to avoid taking any chemistry or physics courses which looked of even medium difficulty. Briefly, the Indi-ana biochemists encouraged me to learn organic chemistry, but after I used a bunsen burner to warm up some benzene, I was relieved from fur-ther true chemistry. It was safer to turn out an uneducated Ph.D. than to risk another explo-sion.[4]

Watson went to Copenhagen to work on DNA. "Journeying abroad initially appeared the perfect solution to the complete lack of chemical facts in my head," he wrote.[5] Bored and restless there, Watson wangled the funds to escape the clouds and cold of Denmark to work at the marine zoological station in sunny Naples, Italy. He was cruelly disappointed. Still cold, this time from the lack of central heating, he found that he had not the slightest interest in marine mammals. "Most of my time I spent walking the streets or reading journal articles from the early days of genetics. Sometimes I daydreamed about discovering the secret of the gene, but not once did I have the faintest trace of a respectable idea."[6]

Then Watson attended a lecture given by Maurice Wilkins of King's College, London. Wilkins had a "picture" of DNA. It was not an ordinary picture, but the swirl of light and dark spots created when X rays pass through the DNA molecule. Although Watson knew nothing about the process—called *X-ray diffraction crystallog-raphy*—the picture excited him.

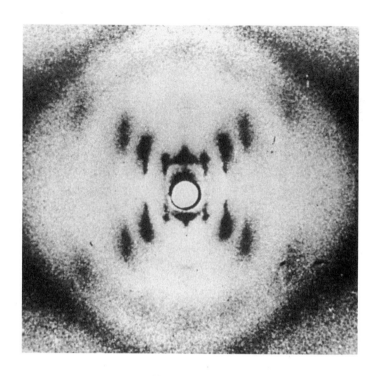

X-ray crystallography images of the
DNA molecule, taken from the top, first
revealed the double helix design.

Watson talked himself into a place at the Cavendish Laboratory in Cambridge, England. There he "immediately discovered the fun of talking to Francis Crick,"[7] a 35-year-old graduate student who had, in the view of his professors, spent too many years working on a Ph.D. dissertation that was still unfinished. Crick's lively personality housed a penetrating intellect that immediately attracted Watson. Besides, Crick knew how to make sense of the beguiling X-ray pictures of DNA.

BUILDING THE HELIX

The pair set out building models of DNA, first with paper and cardboard, later with bits of metal and wire akin to Tinkertoys. They knew that their model had to explain what was known about DNA. It contains molecules of sugar and phosphate. It also contains four molecules called *bases*. The bases are named adenine, thymine, guanine, and cytosine—A, T, G, and C for short. They suspected that the molecule was built like a ladder with sugars and phosphates providing the side supports and the bases linked across the rungs. From previous work done by Edwin Chargaff at Columbia University, they knew that the amounts of A and T were always about equal, as were the amounts of G and C. Watson and Crick took this to mean that A and T always paired. G and C must always pair as well. X-ray pictures suggested that DNA was twisted in a spiral shape called a *helix*.

Wilkins was still working in London. Better and better X-ray pictures, taken by a brilliant crystallographer named Rosalind Franklin, were coming out of his lab. Personalities clashed. "Rosy" thought model building was frivolous. Watson and Crick thought it a shortcut to fame and fortune.

After several embarrassing miscalculations, Watson and Crick finally created a model that explained what Rosalind Franklin's pictures could only hint at. Convinced he was right, Watson nonetheless feared Rosy's response to the completed model. He wrote, "Rosy's instant acceptance of our model at first amazed me. I had feared that

Figure 11: The double helix

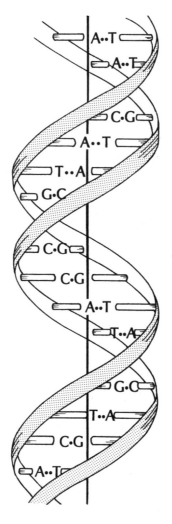

Watson and Crick saw DNA as a spiral staircase.
Sugar and phosphate molecules spiral around
the outside, like supports on a ladder. The
bases form steps or rungs.

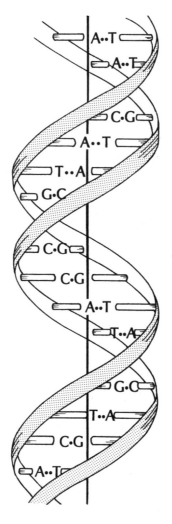

her sharp, stubborn mind . . . might dig up irrelevant results that would foster uncertainty about the correctness of the double helix. Nonetheless, like almost everyone else, she saw the appeal of the base pairs and accepted the fact that the structure was too pretty not to be true."[8]

AT LAST, THE QUESTION IS ANSWERED

There it was in Watson and Crick's model—the answer to that elusive, almost mystical question: "How can life reproduce itself?" It was the A's with the T's and the G's with the C's that did it. Pull apart the two strands of the double helix and make a new strand on each side. An A on the old strand is paired only with a T on the new strand (or vice versa), and a G on the old strand is paired only with a C on the new strand (or vice versa). *The result is two new double helices exactly like the original one.* Life—at the molecular level—has reproduced itself.

Not every scientist jumped at the Watson and Crick model. Geneticists seemed to like the idea, but many prominent biochemists were not impressed. Chargaff at Columbia, whose data about base pairing were so central to the model, thought the whole business a load of nonsense. It took thousands of painstaking experiments to fill in all the pieces of the puzzle Watson and Crick had outlined. Scientists needed another 13 years after Watson and Crick's model to work out the details of how DNA does its job.

Figure 12: DNA copies itself

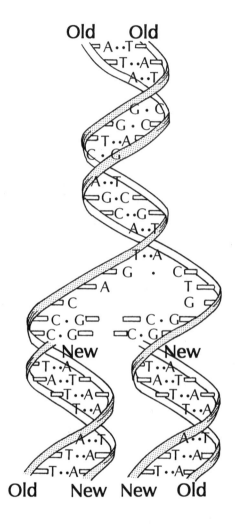

Old   Old

A··T
T··A
A··T
G · C
G · C
T··A
C · G
A··T
G·C
C··G
A·T
T·A
G · C
A   T
C   G
C · G   C · G
C · G   C · G
New   New
T··A   T··A
A··T   A··T
T··A   T··A
T··A   T··A
A··T   A··T
T··A   T··A
T··A   T··A

Old   New   New   Old

Two identical molecules form from the original.
A always pairs with T, and G always pairs with C.

66

PROTEINS

Completing the picture requires a look at another very important class of molecule—the *proteins*. Some are called *structural proteins*. They are the bricks and mortar of life. Flo Hyman's long, lean body and Gregor Mendel's short, round one were built mostly of structural proteins.

Enzymes are another important class of proteins. They are not the bricks and mortar of the living body, but the tool kit. Enzymes work inside every cell speeding up all the chemical changes that make life possible. Reactions that happen only very slowly or at very high temperatures in the test tube can occur quickly at the much lower temperature of the living body because enzymes speed things along. In the cell's *mitochondria*, enzymes release energy from food, making movement and growth possible. Enzymes keep the heart pumping blood, the lungs absorbing oxygen, and nerve cells sending messages throughout the body.

Although every protein is different, they are all built in the same fashion. Proteins are big molecules made from smaller molecules called *amino acids*. There are 20 kinds of amino acids. They have names like serine, threonine, and alanine. Each kind of protein has a unique lineup of amino acids. That lineup determines how the protein will bend and twist into its three-dimensional shape. That shape makes a protein fit with other kinds of molecules, letting it do the job it does. *Thus the number, order and arrangement of amino acids determine what a protein is and does.* For example, the enzyme in the mouth that changes starches into sugars is called amylase. Amylase is the protein it is—and does the job that it does—because of the number, kind, and order of the amino acids that make it. No other protein is the same.

DNA is the blueprint for making proteins. DNA tells the cell what proteins to make and when to make them. Proteins, in turn, do the work of the cell. When proteins are missing or incorrectly constructed, they don't do their jobs properly; that's a genetic disease.

Perhaps you see several complexities here. First, how can DNA direct the manufacture of proteins? DNA is a nucleic acid made of sugar, phosphates, and bases. Proteins are made of amino acids. Somehow, one kind of chemical has to direct the manufacture of another.

Another complexity is the location of DNA. DNA is in the chromosomes, and chromosomes stay inside the cell's nucleus. Proteins are made on structures in the cytoplasm called *ribosomes*. DNA doesn't travel. Somehow the plan for making a protein must move from the nucleus to the ribosome. Clearly, DNA must have some way of sending messages.

CODE, SEND, TRANSLATE

These complexities are not impossible to sort out. To do so, imagine what things must have been like over a century ago, before telephones and fax machines. Suppose you lived in Philadelphia and you

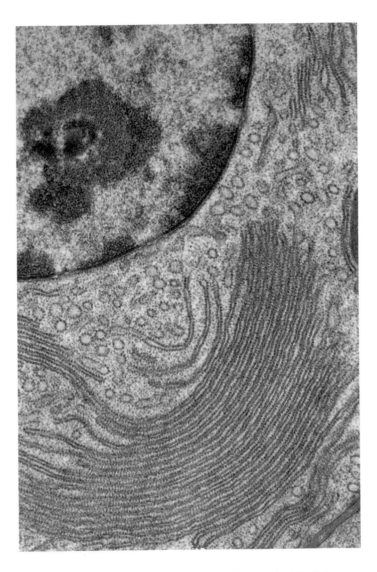

Inside a cell: The nucleus is in the top half of the photo. The parallel lines in the lower half mark a cell structure called the endoplasmic reticulum. Proteins are manufactured at the ribosomes, the black dots lined up in the endoplasmic reticulum.

69

wanted to send a message to a friend in Montreal, a message too important to send through the slow-moving mail system. Your only other choice was to send a telegraph message. In the days before the telephone was invented, telegraph lines (that is, electric wires) could not transmit voices, only clicks—the dots and dashes of Morse code.

Imagine that your situation was even more complicated. Your friend could speak no English, only French. Your message in English first had to be coded into Morse code, transmitted, and then decoded into French. Three steps would be required: *code, send,* and *translate.*

DNA uses these same three steps to direct ribosomes to make proteins. First, the double strand of DNA unzips, exposing the bases that make up the alphabet of the genetic code—A, T, G, and C. The first step is to make a messenger to send to the ribosome. Another kind of nucleic acid called *mRNA* (messenger ribonucleic acid) is made in the nucleus along the single strand of exposed bases on DNA. Remember that in DNA, A always pairs with T and G always pairs with C. Things work the same way for RNA, except there is a U (for uracil) in place of the T. Thus U pairs with A just as T does in DNA.

Figure 13b shows how DNA controls the order of bases on mRNA. The first base on the DNA strand in this example is A. That means the first base on the mRNA is U. Next on DNA comes G, so the next on the mRNA is C. Each base is matched to its partner in turn. This is the first step: *code.*

Once the mRNA strand forms, it travels. That's the *send* part of the process. The mRNA moves out

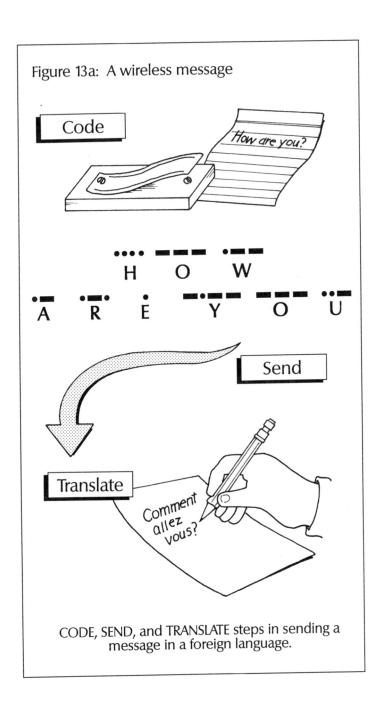

Figure 13a: A wireless message

Code

How are you?

•••• ▬▬▬ •▬▬
H O W

•▬ •▬• • ▬•▬▬ ▬▬• ••▬
A R E Y O U

Send

Translate

Comment allez vous?

CODE, SEND, and TRANSLATE steps in sending a
message in a foreign language.

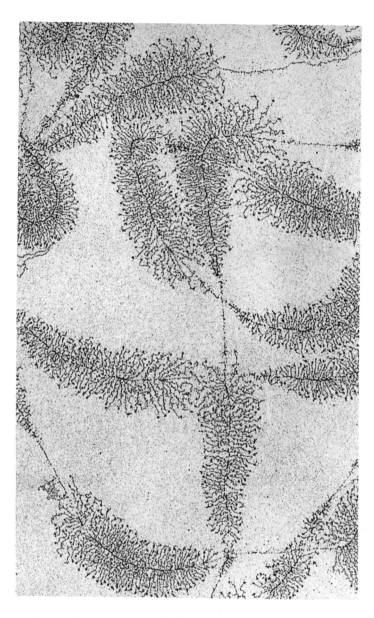

In a cell nucleus, multiple strands of RNA develop
like tree branches along single strands of DNA.

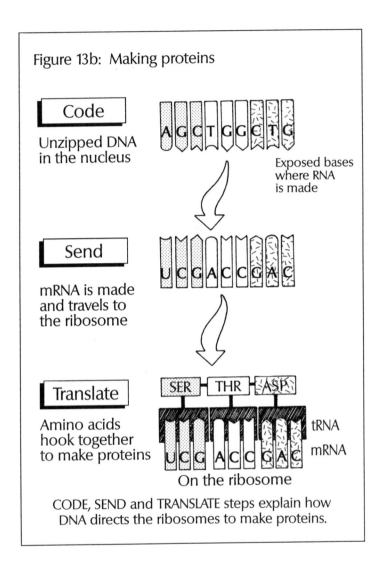

Figure 13b: Making proteins

Code

Unzipped DNA
in the nucleus

AGCTGGCTG

Exposed bases
where RNA
is made

Send

mRNA is made
and travels to
the ribosome

UCGACCGAC

Translate

SER — THR — ASP

Amino acids
hook together
to make proteins

UCG ACC GAC

tRNA

mRNA

On the ribosome

CODE, SEND and TRANSLATE steps explain how
DNA directs the ribosomes to make proteins.

of the nucleus to the ribosome. There, another kind of RNA gets into the act. Transfer RNA molecules, called *tRNA*, carry amino acids. They float around in the cytoplasm of the cell with amino acids attached just waiting for instructions from mRNA.

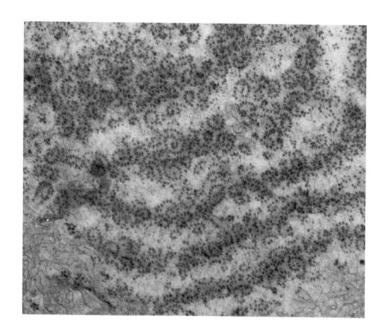

Outside the nucleus, ribosomes and
messenger RNA form spiral patterns.

Next comes the *translation* of the DNA code
into a protein. There is at least one particular kind
of tRNA for each of the 20 amino acids. Each kind
of tRNA molecule can attach to one of the *three letter
codes* on mRNA (see Table 2). When it does, it
brings its amino acid into position to hook up with
another amino acid *in the correct order determined by the
DNA*. When these two amino acids line up side by
side, enzymes help form a bond between them. The
three-letter codes are like words. Each one stands
for a particular amino acid. There are even three-
letter codes that tell the ribosome where to *start* and
stop on the mRNA strand.

74

These processes occur because each molecule has a unique shape determined by the arrangement of atoms of carbon, hydrogen, oxygen, nitrogen, and a few other simple elements. The DNA and mRNA fit together like pieces of a jigsaw puzzle. In the same way, tRNA molecules line up in the right place on the mRNA because their shape fits the three-letter code. Amino acids bond together because of the arrangement of atoms at their exposed ends.

Chains continue to build on a ribosome until many hundreds or thousands of amino acids join.

THE mRNA CODES FOR 20 AMINO ACIDS

First Letter	Second Letter				Third Letter
	U	C	A	G	
U	Phenylalanine	Serine	Tyrosine	Cysteine	U
	Phenylalanine	Serine	Tyrosine	Cysteine	C
	Leucine	Serine	Stop	Stop	A
	Leucine	Serine	Stop	Tryptophan	G
C	Leucine	Proline	Histidine	Arginine	U
	Leucine	Proline	Histidine	Arginine	C
	Leucine	Proline	Glutamine	Arginine	A
	Leucine	Proline	Glutamine	Arginine	G
A	Isoleucine	Threonine	Asparagine	Serine	U
	Isoleucine	Threonine	Asparagine	Serine	C
	Isoleucine	Threonine	Lysine	Arginine	A
	Methionine*	Threonine	Lysine	Arginine	G
G	Valine	Alanine	Aspartic Acid	Glycine	U
	Valine	Alanine	Aspartic Acid	Glycine	C
	Valine	Alanine	Glutamic Acid	Glycine	A
	Valine	Alanine	Glutamic Acid	Glycine	G

* Also frequently a *start* code.

75

Long strings of amino acids are called *polypeptides*. When polypeptide chains join together and fold in on themselves, a working protein is complete.

By the late 1960s, how DNA might control the processes of a cell was fairly well understood. But what role does inheritance play in making life processes go awry and cause a genetic disorder? Scientists all over the world are now trying to answer that question for many thousands of genetic diseases. To see how the one small piece of the answer was found, we must enter another phase of our journey and visit a remote fishing village in Venezuela and a laboratory in Massachusetts.

CHAPTER FIVE

The Gene Stalkers

A toss of her head sends her mane of yellow hair rippling across her shoulders. She pushes it away heedlessly, focusing unwavering attention on her interviewer. Her eyes signal boundless energy, insatiable curiosity. Meet Nancy Wexler, modern-day gene stalker.

She points to a scar on her right arm, a testament to her research of a genetic disorder in a Venezuelan village. She tells how she donated a sample of her own skin to persuade villagers to do the same:

"We explained that we were trying to find the cause of the disease, and while it might not help them, it could help their children and grandchildren. . . . They really understood that, and I think they soon realized that we meant them no harm. I became sort of like a family friend, with syringe."[1]

HUNTINGTON'S DISEASE

Wexler is a clinical psychologist at Columbia University. She conducts research and counsels families on Huntington's disease (HD). Nancy has good reason to be an expert on the disease. She lost her mother, three uncles, and a grandfather to Huntington's. Because a dominant gene causes HD, Wexler has a 50-50 chance of contracting the disorder herself.

HD is among the cruelest of the enemies within. Until recently, there was no way to predict who would get it and who would not. Perhaps worse, the disease usually does not strike until age 35 or older, when an affected individual may already have had children and passed the gene along. A person (like Nancy) who has a chance of carrying the gene is said to be *at risk*.

She explains:

> The symptoms affect just about everything that makes you human—how you think, move, and feel. It causes uncontrollable, involuntary movements in all parts of the body. It can also cause loss of memory, loss of judgment, loss of capacity to organize oneself. In almost all standard school tests, Huntington's disease patients do very poorly. But they do maintain a social intelligence—an awareness of who they are, where they are, and their social setting. The trauma is that they recognize the loss of their capacities—

Nancy Wexler at the 1993
news conference announcing the identification
of the Huntington's disease gene.

their ability to do the kinds of simple things that gave them an identity and gave them some sense of satisfaction and worth. About one in four HD patients makes a serious suicide attempt. Because of the loss of motor skills, other causes of death are falling, hematomas (blood-filled swellings) resulting from a fall, and choking to death. Patients lose the capacity to swallow and can die of malnutrition. They can also lose the capacity to speak. So even if they understand, they can't communicate. It's a difficult, slow decline.[2]

Until Wexler mounted an all-out effort to find the HD gene, this grim picture loomed large for every child of a parent with the disorder. Her own story differs little from the experiences of the families she counsels.

She was 22 when she got the news. Returning home to Los Angeles after studying abroad on a Fulbright scholarship, she learned that her mother, then 53, had HD. Nancy, her sister, and her father were determined to fight the disease with every weapon available. Her father established the Hereditary Disease Foundation. "It gave us something to hold on to. At the time, we all thought we might find a treatment in time to save my mother. We were pretty naive," Nancy admits.[3]

She became president of the foundation, a nonprofit group dedicated to finding a cure to all hereditary diseases, not just HD. The foundation sponsors workshops where scientists meet patients suffering from genetic diseases. Wexler says that the idea of using DNA markers to find the HD gene was born at one of these workshops.

SEARCH FOR A MARKER

What is a DNA marker? Just what it sounds like. It is a piece of DNA that shows up in a particular spot on a chromosome. Scientists find markers by analyzing the chromosomes of as many generations of a family as possible. If the marker shows up in many individuals who also have HD, scientists guess that the marker and the gene are *linked*—that is, they are close together on the same chromosome.

Wexler's search for a marker took her to a fishing village on the shores of Lake Maracaibo in Venezuela. A physician named Americo Negrette reported the disease in the village of San Luis in 1954. At first, he thought the people were drunk all the time because of their uncontrolled body movements and slurred speech. After collecting careful family histories, he realized he was wrong. Large numbers of the villagers were actually sick with HD. The village provided the perfect opportunity for genetic research because families were large and closely related. For example, Nancy found one man who had 29 children from two mothers, and the two mothers were first cousins.

She found the citizens of San Luis ignorant about the disorder. They thought no one in the world was affected except them. Outsiders mocked them. They were known in their region as *sandigteros,* meaning "diseased ones."

Wexler fought resistance to her efforts to collect skin and blood samples and record family trees. The villagers didn't understand why she was there, and they despised giving blood. She stuck with it, making friends, calling town meetings. Eventually, she persuaded over 9,000 people to participate in her research. She calls her work "the most fantastic detective story in the entire world."[4]

After four years of fieldwork, all those blood samples and family trees paid off. In 1983, James Gusella and his co-workers at Massachusetts General Hospital reported finding a marker that placed the HD gene at the tip of chromosome 4. So promising was this piece of good luck that Gusella predicted finding the gene in only five years.

HIDE AND SEEK

Gusella's luck ran out, and so, apparently, had the luck of the other five groups in the United States, England, and Wales who had banded together to track down the Huntington's gene. They knew that the segment of DNA hiding the Huntington's gene was about 6 million bases long. That's far too long a stretch to examine base by base, and the attempt to narrow the search proved futile for a long time. The gene stalkers kept finding people who clearly had HD but lacked the marker. The disease itself didn't give them any help either. No one had any idea what biochemical process leads to the death of brain cells seen in HD patients. Genes are hard enough to find, but if you don't know what a gene does, it is even harder. Wexler called it "the long day's journey into night" as workers slogged wearily on.[5] HD researchers had to watch from the sidelines as other scientists succeeded in finding disease

The team that found the HD gene was led
by James Gusella, shown here with other gene
stalkers from his lab (from left): Mabel Duyao,
Marcy MacDonald, and Christine Ambrose.

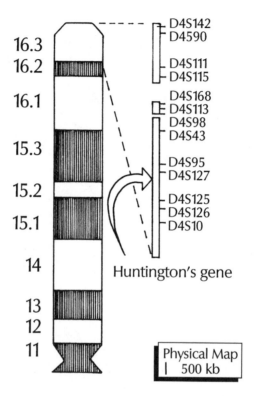

Figure 14: Locating the HD gene

This genetic map shows one arm of chromosome 4. The numbers on the left are band numbers. (Light and dark bands show up when chromosomes are treated with special stains.) On the right is a detail of the light band at the chromosome's tip, with numbers indicating known markers. The arrow shows where the HD gene was found.

genes while their quarry remained stubbornly elusive.

After ten years of painstaking research, the hunt finally ended where it began—in James Gusella's laboratory. On March 26, 1993, Gusella shared with 57 other scientists on both sides of the Atlantic the much deserved glory for finding the gene. It lies on chromosome 4 about 3.5 million base pairs from the tip of what scientists call the "short arm." They named the gene *IT15*. IT stands for "interesting transcript," an honest label, since scientists had no idea what the gene does. The next step was to see what protein the normal gene makes, then learn how that protein is changed in an HD patient.

MUTATION

The HD gene, like all genes that cause disease, must be different from the normal gene; otherwise, there would be no disease. Thus, what scientists must look for is a *mutation*—that is, a change in a gene. A change in a gene means some change in the order of bases—A, T, G, and C. If even a single base changes, the DNA code is different. That means the wrong mRNA forms and the wrong protein is made.

The simplest kinds of mutations are changes in one or more bases. This can happen in three ways. One is *substitution*. That happens when one base accidentally replaces another. A substitution muta- tion causes sickle-cell anemia. Only one three-letter code is different, but that's enough to put a valine where a glutamic acid should be in one part of the hemoglobin molecule. That single amino acid difference means the hemoglobin does not carry oxygen properly.

Another kind of mutation is *insertion*. One or several extra bases get into the DNA, thus changing the three-letter codes all down the line. The third kind is *deletion*, when one or more bases get left out. That changes all the three-letter codes that come after it too.

What causes mutations? Some just happen by chance. Others result from exposure to radiation or toxic chemicals. Mutations are one good reason to worry about the quality of the environment. Pollution can trigger unpredictable changes in DNA and cause birth defects. Gene changes also cause cancer.

The Huntington's gene turns out not to be a simple, single-base mutation. It is what scientists call a *trinucleotide repeat*. The Huntington's mutation is a repetition of the bases CAG near the beginning of the *IT*15 gene. CAG codes for the amino acid glutamine. What's startling is that the number of repeats determines the disease. Gusella's team found 173 people who had between 11 and 34 CAG repeats, and they were all healthy. But people with Huntington's disease had between 42 and about 100 repeats. Scientists guess that this may explain why some people get Huntington's disease while still very young, while others are unaffected until mid-life or even old age. It's possible that the more repeats a person has, the sooner the symptoms of the disease appear.

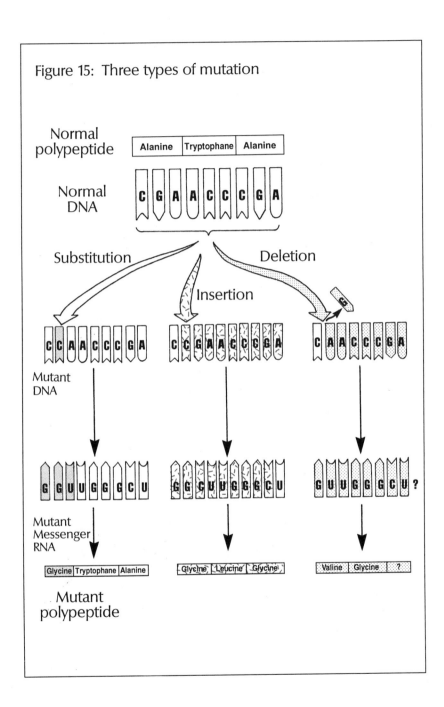

Figure 15: Three types of mutation

MATTERS OF THE HEAD AND HEART

Finding a gene may involve journeys into villages and laboratories. But the information the search yields is a matter for the head and the heart. Now that the gene for HD has been found, people at risk can be tested to learn whether the gene is present before symptoms appear. Imagine yourself at risk. Would *you* want to know if you had the gene? Many people do not, as Nancy explains:

> The availability of the test has provoked people to consider in earnest what it would be like to know that you are going to die at some unspecified time of a degenerative disease of the mind and body. You want to know that you don't have the disease. You don't necessarily want to know that you do have the disease, and you can't risk hearing one answer without the risk of hearing the other. . . . Many people have decided not to take the test until there is a treatment. But there are pressing reasons for taking the test. People may want to know that their children are free of the disease.[6]

Questions also arise about the rights of individuals to privacy, fairness, and nondiscrimination. Among the most sensitive areas are employment and health insurance. Remember, HD rarely affects children. Symptoms usually appear in midlife. If a person is tested for the gene, should the results be given to employers and insurance companies?

Look at these questions first from the point of view of an employer or an insurer. A business may not want to invest in training a person who will get sick and die within a few years. They may not want to pay health insurance premiums for an employee who will need thousands of dollars' worth of medical care. Insurance companies want to eliminate such individuals from the "pool" of insured persons. The idea behind health insurance is sharing risk. When the risk is spread across large numbers of people, only a few of whom actually get sick, then costs can be kept low. People who are sure to get sick are a drain on funds. They are certain to take more out than they put in. Insurers want only healthy people on their rolls if at all possible.

Now look at the questions from the point of view of a person who carries the Huntington's gene. Do such individuals not have a right to happy, productive lives for as long as they stay well? Is it right to deny them work now simply because they will become ill in the future? What about the right to medical care? Should victims of genetic disease be left with no money to pay for the health services they so desperately need? They have a genetic disease through no fault of their own, yet their risk is known. Is that any different from joining the insurance pool with someone else who may die in an automobile accident (also through no fault of his own), the threat of which is *not* known?

Nancy Wexler believes that new knowledge in genetics will expand the number and kind of such questions. She also believes that we need to re-define genetic disorders. She says, "All of us are at risk for something. . . . You can't single out any particular person to be discriminated against. . . . If you start kicking out everybody that has some genetic susceptibility, then you're going to be in tough shape because you don't know who to hire. There won't be anybody left."[7]

She makes a good point. Each of us carries perhaps hundreds of possibly harmful genes. Some never show up because they are recessives present in a single dose. Others make us susceptible to the common killers, heart attacks and cancer. Still others, such as manic-depressive disorders, interact with the environment in complex ways to rob otherwise healthy individuals of happiness.

Such facts fuel the continuing debate of "nature versus nurture." How much of our behavior, intellect, and personality comes from our genes? How much is the product of our environment? Debates of this sort have been fueled in recent years by scientific discoveries of a link between certain genes and such personal characteristics as smoking and alcoholism. The controversy is of more than academic interest. Some argue that if "genes are destiny," then maybe it doesn't matter very much how children are raised. Some say that if people are going to come out a certain way no matter what, why spend money on education, nutrition, or social services? People on the other side of the argument say genes are far less important than the love, nurturing, teaching, and care young people receive as they grow.

Steve Jones, professor of genetics at University College in London, maintains that "nature/nurture" is a faulty distinction.

Although genetics is all about inheritance, inheritance is certainly not all about genetics. Nearly all inherited characters more complicated than a single change in the DNA involve gene and environment acting together. It is impossible to sort them into convenient compartments. An attribute such as intelligence is often seen as a cake which can be sliced into so much "gene" and so much "environment." In fact, the two are so closely blended that trying the separate them is more like trying to unbake the cake.[8]

OTHER TARGETS, OTHER STRATEGIES

While debate over these issues continues, scientists are making progress in the search for other disease-causing genes. HD isn't the only gene that has been located. In 1989, Canadian and American researchers announced finding the cystic fibrosis gene spread over a long stretch of DNA (250,000 base pairs) on chromosome 7. Most of that stretch is taken up by inactive regions called *introns*. The real work of coding for a protein is done by 24 separate, active fragments called *exons*. Together the exons code for a protein made of 1,480 amino acids. The protein seems to play a role in controlling the excretion of chloride ions (charged atoms of chlorine) from the cell.

In 70 percent of the CF patients, the protein seems to lack one amino acid, a phenylalanine. Gene stalkers are now trying to find the mutations that occur in the other 30 percent. That discrepancy has slowed efforts to develop a test for carriers of the CF gene.

One way of looking for human genes involves the use of an *animal model*, a variety of animal (usually mice) that shows the same symptoms of a disease as humans. For example, farmers have long noticed that many blue-eyed, all-white cats are deaf. Doctors, too, have noticed that a white forelock and widely spaced eyes in people sometimes accompany an inherited form of deafness called Waardenburg's syndrome. Waardenburg's syndrome accounts for about 2 or 3 percent of the one million cases of inborn deafness reported in the United States every year. Scientists think that they have found a likely explanation for why blue eyes and white hair seem to occur along with deafness in both cats and people.

In the early 1990s, geneticists at six laboratories in three countries were stalking the Waardenburg's gene. Many studied a strain of mice called "Splotch," named for the white patches on the animals' bellies, heads, and tails. In 1991 a Canadian team reported that Splotch mice have a fault in a gene named *Pax-3*. During development of the embryo, this gene stimulates certain cells to develop into skin and the nervous system.

A few months later, English and American teams found a similar mutation among families with Waardenburg's. They called the gene *HuP2*. It seems to influence the embryological development of cells that produce skin, eye, hair, and the inner ear. Finding the gene meant gene stalkers could take the next step—creating a test for deaf couples to see if they carry the gene.

The Marfan's gene was found in 1991, five years too late to help Flo Hyman. The gene resides on chromosome 15. It codes for the protein fibrillin, which, among other things, supports the walls of arteries. Marfan's sufferers either make too little fibrillin or they make a faulty version.

In 1992, doctors performed the first diagnosis of Marfan's before a child was born. A pregnant woman with a mild case wanted to know if her child would also have the disease. Doctors at the Nebraska Medical Center in Omaha inserted a needle into the mother's uterus and took a tissue sample that contained cells from the developing fetus. They grew the cells in the laboratory and looked for the mutation. The test showed that the baby had inherited the faulty gene.

The Marfan's test may also resolve a controversy that is over a century old. Did Abraham Lincoln have the syndrome? There may be enough of Lincoln's DNA in specimens of his blood, hair, and bone at the National Museum of Health and Medicine to answer the question. By 1994, an ethics panel set up to advise the museum had approved a physician's request to test the samples.

The decision set off a flurry of arguments. Those in favor pointed out that Lincoln has no living descendants, so no one's privacy is violated. They felt that testing Lincoln's DNA would generate publicity for Marfan's, which could benefit people who carry the gene. Others disagreed. They believed that genetic testing should never be done without permission from the person tested. Some people consider the research ghoulish, something akin to grave robbing.

Beneath this argument lay an issue no one could dispute. Our understanding of the gene has brought us into a new realm. We can now know an individual's genetic makeup as we never have before. Parents can be forewarned of their children's genetic disorders before birth. And some of those disorders can even be cured. Let's explore this fascinating and controversial area of genetics in the final leg of our journey.

CHAPTER SIX

The Gene Doctors

Kesha Bennett recalls her meeting with a genetic counselor. "I didn't know whether to love him or hate him," Kesha says. "I knew that if he said the right thing, I'd want to hug him, and if he said the wrong thing, I'd want to hit him. It didn't seem right to have such strong feelings toward a perfect stranger, so I just sat there, twisting my fingers in my lap and wishing I could be someplace else."

Kesha is about to be a mother for the first time. She and her husband, Darryl, waited a long time for children. "At first, we just weren't ready. We married right out of college, and we both had our careers," Kesha explains. She's a market research analyst. Darryl runs a construction company. "Later, we started planning a family, but I had trouble getting pregnant. When I finally did get pregnant, I was almost 38." Kesha flashes Darryl a crooked smile. "That's when the doctors descended on us," she says, and Darryl nods.

Darryl picks up the story from there. "First, they said we should be tested for sickle cell because we're both black. There's been screening here for years, you know, testing everyone they can get to come in. I always meant to go, but never quite got around to it. Didn't seem much reason, really. We've never been sick a day in our lives, either of us." A faraway look crosses Darryl's face. "But after Kesha got pregnant I started to pay attention. The doctors said either one of us could carry the gene without being sick. And if we both carried the gene, our child might have sickle-cell anemia."

Kesha interrupts, "We could have refused these tests, of course, but that didn't seem very smart. So once we decided to go ahead, we had to be the world's quickest studies. I haven't had a science class since I was 18 and I don't think Darryl has either. Now, here we are, all of a sudden, becoming genetics experts just because we want a baby."

Darryl continues: "It turned out that I carry the gene but Kesha doesn't, so there's no problem for our kid, except he might carry the gene. So he'll need to be tested someday, he and his wife, to see if their kids might get sickle cell. Complicated, isn't it?"

They laugh.

"No sooner were we through with one test than they said we should have another," Kesha says.

"They explained to us that mothers Kesha's age are more likely to have a baby with Down's syndrome," says Darryl. "They recommended amniocentesis. The ultrasound exam they gave Kesha before the amniocentesis let us see our baby on a television screen. The pictures showed a boy."

"It took a couple of weeks for our test results to come back, and I was nervous the whole time," Kesha adds. "I was so afraid the counselor would tell us there was something wrong with our baby, but the news was good. Our boy will be healthy!"

TESTING FOR DISORDERS

The man whom Kesha feared didn't mean to frighten her. He meant to help. He is one of a growing corps of health professionals called *genetic counselors*. Sometimes genetic counselors are doctors, but often they are people specially trained in genetics and counseling techniques who work closely with doctors in genetics clinics. Their job is to give people the information they need to make decisions about their own health or the health of their unborn children.

Genetic counselors often work with couples like Kesha and Darryl who are at risk because of their ethnic group, age, or family history. Sometimes counselors try to answer the question "Will it happen again?" when parents already have a child with a genetic defect or the disorder is present in other family members. Counselors may also work with adults whose family backgrounds put them at risk for health problems such as breast cancer, diabetes, or Huntington's disease.

Darryl and Kesha had their blood tested to see if they carried the sickle-cell gene, but the test for Down's syndrome required cells from the *fetus*, a term used to describe the developing human organism after about the fourth month of pregnancy. The test does not look for a faulty gene, but for an extra dose of DNA. Children with Down's usually have three copies of chromosome 21 instead of the normal two. As a result, they are short and have sloping eyes and small facial features. Their tongues are usually large and may protrude from the mouth. About a third have some kind of heart disorder, and many develop hearing, speech, or vision problems. All experience some degree of mental retardation and a shortened life span.

Amniocentesis is one way of testing before birth to see if a fetus has Down's syndrome. This procedure is now routinely offered to any woman whose age (35 or older) or family history shows her at risk of having an affected child. It is done around the 15th week of pregnancy. A needle inserted into the uterus draws out a small sample of the fluid that surrounds the fetus. Some fetal cells float in that fluid. Large numbers of those cells are then grown in the laboratory.

Another method of testing is *chorionic villus sampling (CVS)*. A sample of cells is taken from an area of the *placenta*, the structure that nourishes the baby during its nine months of development. Since this part of the placenta grows from the fertilized egg, its cells contain the same chromosomes as the embryo. CVS can be done earlier than amniocentesis, but it carries with it a slightly greater risk of causing a miscarriage.

Whatever method gets cells from the fetus, the test for Down's syndrome is the same. Technicians take pictures of the cell nuclei through a microscope and examine the chromosomes. If the fetus

Figure 16: Down's syndrome

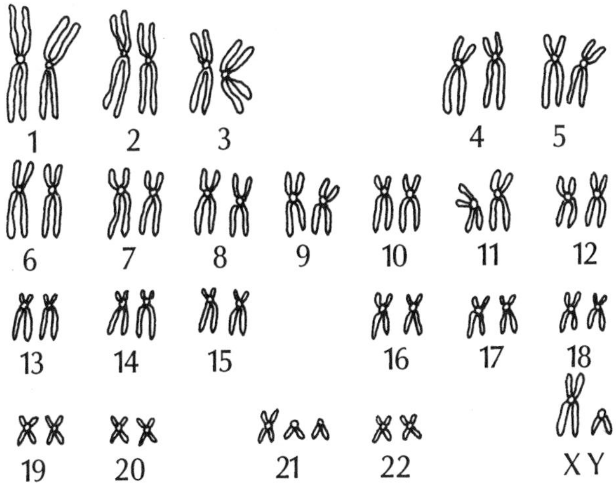

1	2	3		4	5	
6	7	8	9	10	11	12
13	14	15		16	17	18
19	20		21	22		X Y

The chromosomes of a child with Down's
syndrome include an extra copy of
chromosome 21.

carries an extra chromosome 21 or some other ab-
normality of the chromosomes shows up, the
mother can choose whether to end the pregnancy
or carry on and have the child.

Down's syndrome used to affect one or two out
of every 100 babies born, but that number has been
falling in recent years, mostly because older women
are having fewer children.[1] Still, 80 percent of
Down's babies diagnosed in the United States are
born to women younger than 35.[2] That's too many
mothers for everyone to have amniocentesis. Now
a simple blood test is available to pregnant women

99

of all ages. It measures the levels of certain chemicals in the mother's blood that occur in abnormal amounts if she is carrying a child with Down's syndrome or some other birth defects. A suspicious blood test isn't proof on its own. Amniocentesis is still required, but even that may change if a new, even safer procedure is developed that can locate cells from the fetus that occasionally leak into the mother's blood.

Some people balk at the idea of genetic counseling and prenatal testing because many parents who receive a positive test for a disorder such as Down's choose to end the pregnancy. Some who oppose prenatal testing consider abortion wrong under any circumstances. Parents who feel that way may choose not to have prenatal testing. For others who reject abortion, prenatal testing may still be a good idea. Parents who know a handicapped child is on the way may use the time to prepare themselves by learning all they can and planning ways to meet the infant's needs. Others see no moral dilemma in terminating a pregnancy. Some think abortion is justified in certain instances, including rape, incest, threat to the life of the mother, or genetic disease. Still others think it is a woman's right to choose abortion no matter what her reason.

GENE THERAPY

Abortion is a controversial issue in the United States and in some other parts of the world. Until recently, the only way to avoid genetic disease was to prevent the birth of the affected individual. Now, a new kind of medicine is realizing what was once only a dream: *gene therapy*. Researchers are looking for ways to replace or repair damaged genes—or, at least, to keep them from doing their dirty work. The day may come when physicians will be able to offer genetic treatments for disorders once considered incurable.

On September 14, 1990, a four-year-old girl in Cleveland, Ohio, made headlines around the world. She was the first person in history to be "operated on" in a gene therapy experiment. The girl had a rare inherited condition called ADA deficiency. Her body made too little of an enzyme, adenosine deaminase (ADA for short), needed by the immune system. The most famous sufferer of ADA deficiency was David, the "boy in a bubble," who lived inside a plastic dome, isolated from the outside world because his immune system failed to develop. Even the common chicken pox virus can kill a child with ADA deficiency.

David died in 1984, but for the Cleveland girl a new hope materialized. Doctors at the National Institutes of Health removed some of her blood cells, fortified them with healthy copies of her faulty gene, and returned them to her bloodstream. The therapy worked better than anyone had dared expect. In less than a year, the child's immune system was working so well that she was able to attend kindergarten. Gene therapy today is an alternative for ADA-deficient children for whom bone marrow transplants and the "PEG" treatment (administration of the missing enzyme) either don't work or are too risky.

New approaches to gene therapy that have worked in animals offer hope to children with cys-

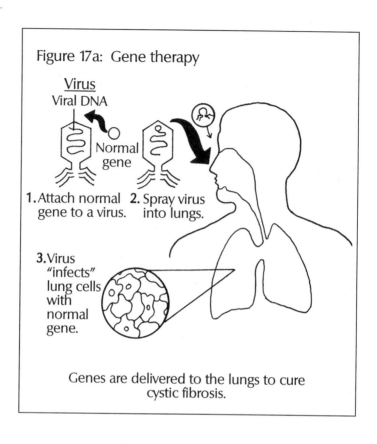

Figure 17a: Gene therapy

Virus
Viral DNA

Normal gene

1. Attach normal gene to a virus. 2. Spray virus into lungs.

3. Virus "infects" lung cells with normal gene.

Genes are delivered to the lungs to cure cystic fibrosis.

tic fibrosis. Doctors splice the normal human genes into some cold viruses that have been altered so they can't reproduce and make the patient sick. Then they spray the viruses containing the normal genes into the lungs. The cold viruses infect the respiratory cells—without causing illness—and insert the normal genes into the nuclei of the lung cells. When all goes as planned, the patient makes a normal mucus that doesn't invite infections.

Gene therapy is also being tested against cancer. Cancer is not one disease but many, all grouped together because of the abnormal ways in which cancer cells behave. Many cancers are cases of uncontrolled cell division. Normal cells "know" when to divide and when not to. Cancer cells keep dividing out of control. Nothing checks their growth. In other cancers, such as leukemia, cell division occurs as it should, but the cells don't mature normally. Cancer cells can also grow in places where they should not. The migration of cancer cells to other parts of the body where they often grow and cause new tumors is called *metastasis*.

In one attempt to fight these mutated cells, doctors first collect white blood cells they find within the patient's tumor. These are the cells of the immune system that have recognized the tumor and are trying to fight it. The researchers then use a virus to "infect" these white cells with the instructions for making a powerful cancer-fighting protein called tumor necrosis factor. The white cells are then grown in large numbers and injected back into patients.

The immune system works by attacking proteins it recognizes as foreign invaders. Cancer cells are a person's own cells. Therefore, some cancer cells have no foreign proteins, so the immune system may fail to fight them. To solve that problem, researchers package genes for foreign proteins in tiny fat globules. The globules slip through cell membranes and drop their payload inside. The idea is for the inserted genes to make foreign proteins that stick to the surface of tumor cells, alerting the immune system to the cancer's presence. Experiments with mice have shown that once the immune system starts to work on the tumor, it will also

103

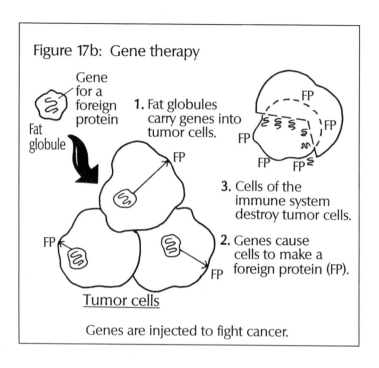

Figure 17b: Gene therapy

Gene for a foreign protein

Fat globule

1. Fat globules carry genes into tumor cells.

3. Cells of the immune system destroy tumor cells.

2. Genes cause cells to make a foreign protein (FP).

Tumor cells

Genes are injected to fight cancer.

track down and kill cancer cells not containing the added gene.

Another way is to introduce a "suicide gene" that makes cancer cells resemble something else. For example, planting a gene from the herpes simplex virus in tumor cells should make them susceptible to treatment with antiherpes drugs.

Yet another idea is to turn the body's cells into miniature drug factories. Some people have a form of diabetes caused by the inability of their pancreas to make enough *insulin*, the substance that regulates the level of sugar in the blood. Transplanting the gene for making insulin into pancreatic cells might cure their disease. Another candidate for this kind of gene therapy is Parkinson's disease. The trembling and unsteady gait of Parkinson's patients may result from a lack of the chemical dopamine in the brain. If genes could direct brain cells to make dopamine, the symptoms might disappear.

For all its promise, gene therapy has its worries. Transplanted genes might turn normal cells into cancers. They could infect the wrong cells, causing them to stop vital functions. Even in the right cells, they might interfere with essential chemical reactions. Most important, gene doctors want to be sure they don't tinker in any way (even unintentionally) with sperm and egg. Modifications of reproductive cells could affect future generations in ways no one can predict.

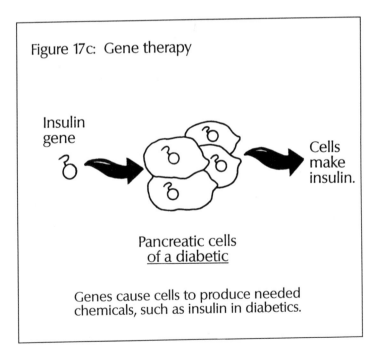

Figure 17c: Gene therapy

Insulin gene

Cells make insulin.

Pancreatic cells of a diabetic

Genes cause cells to produce needed chemicals, such as insulin in diabetics.

Some people even question the whole idea of gene therapy. Is it right to attempt to change life processes at the most basic chemical level? Richard Mulligan, the first scientist to use a virus as a "delivery truck" for genes, believes in a "go slow" approach to gene therapy. He says, "I don't want to be a piece of history that's moved too fast, that's rushed to do things in humans, that's been careless. We want to have a clear idea of the risks and benefits before we give a gene transplant. . . . No maybes. No mysteries."[3]

THE HUMAN
GENOME PROJECT

The maybes and the mysteries are growing fewer each day as the Human Genome Project carries on its work. Governments all over the world have invested billions of dollars in this international effort involving 9,000 scientists in 36 countries. Their goal is to map and sequence all 100,000 genes contained in human DNA. They plan to draw three kinds of gene maps. The first will show the positions of genes on chromosomes. The second will describe the size of each gene—that is, the number of bases that compose it. The third will list the exact sequence of bases in each gene. There are some 3 billion base pairs (that's 6 billion bases!) in human genes. If the base pairs were ever published in a book at 3,000 letters to a page, it would take over 20 years to read it.

Nancy Wexler calls the Human Genome project "the most ambitious, imaginative, daring, and

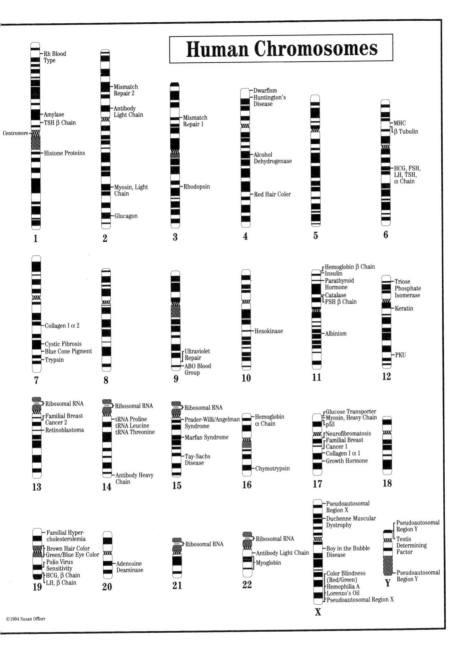

Human Chromosomes

1
- Rh Blood Type
- Amylase
- TSH β Chain
- Centromere
- Histone Proteins

2
- Mismatch Repair 2
- Antibody Light Chain
- Myosin, Light Chain
- Glucagon

3
- Mismatch Repair 1
- Rhodopsin

4
- Dwarfism
- Huntington's Disease
- Alcohol Dehydrogenase
- Red Hair Color

5

6
- MHC
- β Tubulin
- HCG, FSH, LH, TSH, α Chain

7
- Collagen I α 2
- Cystic Fibrosis
- Blue Cone Pigment
- Trypsin

8

9
- Ultraviolet Repair
- ABO Blood Group

10
- Hexokinase

11
- Hemoglobin β Chain
- Insulin
- Parathyroid Hormone
- Catalase
- FSH β Chain
- Albinism

12
- Triose Phosphate Isomerase
- Keratin
- PKU

13
- Ribosomal RNA
- Familial Breast Cancer 2
- Retinoblastoma

14
- Ribosomal RNA
- tRNA Proline
- tRNA Leucine
- tRNA Threonine
- Antibody Heavy Chain

15
- Ribosomal RNA
- Prader-Willi/Angelman Syndrome
- Marfan Syndrome
- Tay-Sachs Disease

16
- Hemoglobin α Chain
- Chymotrypsin

17
- Glucose Transporter
- Myosin, Heavy Chain
- p53
- Neurofibromatosis
- Familial Breast Cancer 1
- Collagen I α 1
- Growth Hormone

18

19
- Familial Hyper-cholesterolemia
- Brown Hair Color
- Green/Blue Eye Color
- Polio Virus Sensitivity
- HCG, β Chain
- LH, β Chain

20
- Adenosine Deaminase

21
- Ribosomal RNA

22
- Ribosomal RNA
- Antibody Light Chain
- Myoglobin

X
- Pseudoautosomal Region X
- Duchenne Muscular Dystrophy
- Boy in the Bubble Disease
- Color Blindness (Red/Green)
- Hemophilia A
- Lorenzo's Oil
- Pseudoautosomal Region X

Y
- Pseudoautosomal Region Y
- Testis Determining Factor
- Pseudoautosomal Region Y

© 1994 Susan Offner

A map of human chromosomes shows the positions of some of the genes that scientists have been able to track down.

foolhardy effort for mankind to know itself that anyone has ever attempted." She says, "The real hope is that by learning where the genes are we will understand what they do. I think this will have profound implications for our own understanding of how we function, how we're put together, how we interact with each other, and how we interact with the environment."[4]

Already two complete chromosomes—the Y and number 21—have been taken apart and put back together again. This research has produced a set of overlapping pieces of DNA assembled in the correct order. That kind of map is still a long way from sequencing every single base, but it helps scientists find genes more quickly. Each day brings new discoveries and new surprises as scientists venture farther and father into the uncharted territory of genetics.

CONCLUSION

Memories of Your Journey

As with any journey, you return home with your memories—the best possible souvenirs from any trip. What will you remember most about your brief excursion into the vast territory of genetics?

Will you marvel over the intricacies of that living machine called the cell and its master control molecule, DNA? Will you gaze again at your mental snapshot of that busy factory called the ribosome, where the proteins that make living things work are manufactured?

Will you recall fondly the people you have met? There was Gregor Mendel, who died never knowing he would someday be acclaimed as the Father of Genetics. There was Robert, nicknamed Bobby, who puts up with arduous physical therapy in hopes of being a sports reporter someday. And what about Nancy Wexler, who lost her mother to a killer disease and fought back by searching for the gene that causes it?

You may remember the pauses you made along the way to consider questions of right and wrong. Have you asked yourself whether *you* would want to know if you carried the Huntington's gene? Would you want your employer to know, or your insurance company? What about the gene doctors? In your view are they right in their attempts to repair faulty genes, or should nature be left to its own devices? Have you wondered how far gene therapy might go? Could it go too far?

Perhaps you recognize now how useful your maps were in guiding you through the terrain called genetics. The patterns of inheritance you encountered—including dominant, recessive, and sex-linked—gave you some clues about what to expect along the way. Your knowledge of the three-letter code in DNA showed you how genes work.

Perhaps you now realize, however, how incomplete those maps are. There is still so much to learn—so much territory to explore—but for that new journey, you will need to set off on your own. You know the major landmarks now. Further reading and research will lead you to greater understanding as you progress.

This brief journey is over, but your exploration of genetics has only begun.

NOTES

CHAPTER 1

1. Ken Denlinger, "U.S. Women Find a Silver Lining," *Washington Post*, August 9, 1984, p. E1.
2. Ibid.
3. Ibid., p. E6.
4. Teri Randall, "Marfan Syndrome Gene Search Intensifies Following Identification of Basic Defect," *Journal of the American Medical Association* 264 (1990), p. 1642.
5. Reader's Digest Association, *The ABC's of the Human Body: A Family Answer Book* (Pleasantville, N.Y.: Reader's Digest, 1992), p. 22.
6. Yvonne Baskin, "DNA Unlimited," *Discover* 11, no. 7 (July 1990), pp. 77–79.
7. George Vecsey, "Remembering Flo Hyman," *New York Times*, February 5, 1988, p. 25.

CHAPTER 2

1. Hugo Iltis, *Life of Mendel* (London: George Allen and Unwin Ltd, 1932), p. 47.
2. Gregor Mendel, "Experiments in Plant Hybridization," *Proceedings of the Brno Society for the Study of Natural Science*, 1866.

CHAPTER 3

1. C. Ezzell, "Gene Therapy for Cystic Fibrosis Patients," *Science News* 142, no. 24 (December 12, 1992), p. 405.
2. T.M.B., "Winning Candidate: A Painstaking Search Identifies the Gene for Cystic Fibrosis," *Scientific American* 261, no. 5 (November 1989), pp. 28–30.
3. Walter A. Schroeder, Edwin S. Munger, and Darleen R. Powars, "Sickle Cell Anemia, Genetic Variations, and the Slave Trade to the United States," *Journal of African History* 3, no. 2 (1990), pp. 163–180.

CHAPTER 4

1. James D. Watson, *The Double Helix* (New York: Atheneum, 1968), p. 205.
2. Leon Jaroff, "Happy Birthday, Double Helix," *Time* 141, no. 11 (March 15, 1993), pp. 56–59.
3. Stephen Hall, "Old School Ties: Watson, Crick, and 40 Years of DNA," *Science* 259, no. 5101 (March 12, 1993), pp. 1532–1533.

4. Watson, pp. 21–22.
5. Ibid., p. 22.
6. Ibid., p. 30.
7. Ibid., p. 48.
8. Ibid., p. 210.

CHAPTER 5

1. Leon Jaroff, "Making the Best of a Bad Gene," *Time* 139, no. 6 (February 10, 1992), pp. 78–79.

2. Neil A. Campbell, "A Conversation with Nancy Wexler," *American Biology Teacher* 52, no. 74 (February 1990), pp. 74–79.

3. Jaroff, p. 78.

4. Campbell, p. 76.

5. Leslie Roberts, "The Huntington's Gene Quest Goes On," *Science* 258, no. 5083 (October 30, 1992), pp. 740–741.

6. Campbell, p. 77.

7. Ibid., p. 78.

8. Steve Jones, *The Language of the Genes: Biology, History, and the Evolutionary Future* (London: HarperCollins, 1993), p. 171.

CHAPTER 6

1. "Declining Mortality from Down Syndrome—No Cause for Complacency," *Lancet* 335, no. 8694 (April 14, 1990), pp. 888–889.

2. "Down's Syndrome: Blood Put to the Test," *Good Housekeeping* 216, no. 4 (April 1993), p. 48.

3. Geoffrey Montgomery, "The Ultimate Medicine," *Discover* 11, no. 3 (March 1990), pp. 60–68.

4. Neil A. Campbell, "A Conversation with Nancy Wexler," *American Biology Teacher* 52, no. 74 (February 1990), p. 78.

GLOSSARY

amino acids   The building blocks of proteins.

amniocentesis   A medical procedure that removes a sample of the fluid surrounding a fetus in order to obtain fetal cells for genetic testing.

animal model   Any strain of animals (usually mice) that show symptoms of a disease similar to those observed in humans. Useful for research.

antibodies   Infection-fighting molecules made by the immune system.

at risk   Describes a person who has a chance of carrying a gene for a hereditary disorder because of family history, but does not know for sure.

bases   One of four molecules that form the rungs of the DNA ladder and make the genetic code: adenine (A), thymine (T), guanine (G), and cytosine (C).

carrier   An individual possessing one recessive gene in a gene pair. Usually refers to those having a gene for a genetic disorder.

cell The basic unit from which most living things are made.

cell membrane The thin layer that forms the boundary of an animal cell. The membrane holds the cell together and regulates what substances can enter and leave a cell.

chorionic villus sampling (CVS) A procedure that takes fetal cells for genetic testing from a part of the placenta.

chromosomes Bodies in the nucleus that contain genes. Genes are pieces of DNA. Chromosomes may be thought of as strings of genes.

cytoplasm The jellylike material that forms most of the cell.

deletion The kind of mutation in which one or more bases is dropped from DNA.

DNA Deoxyribonucleic acid. The molecule that makes up the gene.

dominant A gene that shows its effects when only one member of the gene pair is the gene in question. Also, the pattern of inheritance in which a characteristic associated with a dominant gene shows up in every generation.

embryo An organism in its early stages of development.

enzymes Proteins that speed up chemical reactions in cells.

exons Active portions of DNA that make up a gene.

family tree A drawing showing parents and children over several generations.

116

fertilization   The union of egg and sperm.

fetus   A human embryo after the third month of pregnancy.

gene   The basic unit of heredity. A piece of DNA that codes for a string of amino acids needed to make a protein.

gene therapy   Medical procedures that seek to repair or replace damaged genes or block their action.

genetic counselor   A health professional who advises people on medical matters associated with inheritance.

genetics   The study of inheritance.

helix   A spiral-shaped molecule. DNA has two spiral strands. Therefore, it is called a double helix.

hemoglobin   The protein in the blood that carries oxygen.

insertion   The kind of mutation in which one or more bases is added to DNA.

insulin   The substance made by the pancreas that regulates levels of sugar in the blood.

intron   Inactive regions of DNA that must be removed before exons join together to form a working gene.

linked   Describes genes that are close together on the same chromosome.

metastasis   The migration of cancer cells from one part of the body to another.

mitochondria   The powerhouses of the cell where energy from food is released.

molecule   An assembly of atoms.

mRNA   Messenger RNA. Formed from the blueprint

117

of DNA in the nucleus, mRNA travels to the ribosomes, where it directs the manufacture of proteins.

multifactorial Describes a characteristic determined by both gene and environment.

mutation A change in a gene. May be caused by chance, chemicals, radiation, or other environmental hazards.

nucleus The dense body inside the cytoplasm of the cell where DNA is contained in chromosomes.

organism Any living thing.

pistil The female reproductive structure of the flower; it contains eggs.

placenta The structure that nourishes the fetus and removes waste during prenatal development.

polygenic Describes a characteristic determined by many genes.

polypeptide A chain of amino acids.

protein One or more polypeptides joined together and folded into a three-dimensional shape.

recessive A gene that does not show its effects unless both members of the gene pair are the same (this does not apply for sex-linked genes). Also, the pattern of inheritance associated with a recessive gene.

ribosome The structure in the cell where proteins are made.

RNA Ribonucleic acid. A molecule similar to DNA, except that the sugar is different and RNA contains uracil instead of thymine.

sex chromosomes The 23d pair of chromosomes in humans. Most females have two X chromosomes. Most males have an X and a Y.

sex-linked Describes a gene carried on the X chromosome, or the pattern of inheritance associated with a gene carried on the X chromosome.

stamen The male reproductive structure of a flower; it produces pollen.

structural proteins Proteins that build the bodies of organisms.

substitution The kind of mutation in which one base is inserted in place of another.

trinucleotide repeat The kind of mutation in which a series of three bases is copied too many times.

tRNA Transfer RNA. Its function is to ferry amino acids into place as proteins are built on ribosomes.

X-ray diffraction crystallography A way of using X rays to take "pictures" of molecules.

BOOKS

British Medical Association. *Our Genetic Future: The Science and Ethics of Genetic Technology.* New York: Oxford University Press, 1992. A hard look at the science behind gene engineering, with an equally close examination of the rights and wrongs of biotechnology.

Chicago Tribune. Altered Fates: The Promise of Gene Therapy. Reprinted by Department of Health and Human Services, PHS–National Institutes of Health, 1986. A newspaper-style introduction to the promises of gene therapy, from the mapping of genes to the eradication of cancer.

Crick, Francis. *What Mad Pursuit: A Personal View of Scientific Discovery.* New York: Basic Books, 1988. Francis Crick reminisces about his life and what he sees as the classical period of molecular genetics, from 1953, when he and Watson modeled the structure of DNA, until 1966, when the genetic code was finally cracked.

Gonick, Larry, and Mark Wheelis. *The Cartoon Guide of Genetics.* New York: HarperCollins, 1991. Learn genetics the easy way—from cartoons.

Hall, Stephen S. *Invisible Frontiers: The Race to Synthesize a Human Gene.* New York: Atlantic Monthly Press, 1987. Competition was keen as scientists and laboratories vied to be first to make a working gene in a test tube.

Shapiro, Robert. *The Human Blueprint: The Race to Unlock the Secrets of Our Genetic Script.* New York: St. Martin's Press, 1991. The story of the Human Genome Project.

Watson, James D. *The Double Helix: A Personal Account of the Discovery of the Structure of DNA.* New York: Atheneum, 1968. When brash young Jim Watson left Indiana for Europe, he dreamed of foreign girls to be puzzled over, wines to be tasted, politics to be argued. Oh, yes, along the way, he hoped to unlock the secrets of the gene.

Wingerson, Lois. *Mapping Our Genes: The Genome Project and the Future of Medicine.* New York: Dutton, 1990. A nonscientist looks inside the lives and work of some extraordinary gene stalkers.

MAGAZINE ARTICLES

Demak, Richard. "Marfan Syndrome: A Silent Killer." *Sports Illustrated,* February 17, 1986, pp. 30–35.

Diamond, Jared. "Curse and Blessing of the Ghetto." *Discover,* March 1991, pp. 60–65. Tay-Sachs disease.

Elmer-Dewitt, Philip. "The Genetic Revolution." *Time,* January 17, 1994, pp. 32–39.

Jaroff, Leon. "Happy Birthday, Double Helix." *Time*, March 15, 1993, pp. 56–59.

Jaroff, Leon. "Making the Best of a Bad Gene." *Time*, February 10, 1992, pp. 78–79. Nancy Wexler's story.

Lowenstein, Jerold M. "Genetic Surprises." *Discover*, December 1992, pp. 82–88.

Lowenstein, Jerold M. "The Remaking of the President." *Discover*, August 1991, pp. 18–20. Testing Abraham Lincoln's DNA for Marfan's.

Merz, Beverly. "Designer Genes." *American Health*, March 1993, pp. 46–54.

Montgomery, Geoffrey. "The Ultimate Medicine." *Discover*, March 1990, pp. 60–68.

Ravage, Barbara. "Medical Genetics: A Brave New World." *Current Health 2*, February 1993, pp. 6–12.

FREE PAMPHLETS

Inside the Cell

The Office of Research Reports
National Institutes of Health
Building 31, Room 4 A 52
Baltimore, MD 20892

What You Should Know About
Jewish Genetic Diseases

National Foundation for Jewish Genetic Disease
250 Park Avenue, Suite 1000
New York, NY 10177

122

Is a Career in Genetic Counseling in Your Future?

National Society of Genetic Counselors, Inc.
233 Canterbury Drive
Wallingford, PA 19086

Solving the Puzzle: Careers in Genetics

American Society of Human Genetics
Administrative Office
9650 Rockville Pike
Bethesda, MD 2081

Sickle Cell Anemia Fact Sheet

Sickle Cell Disease Association of America
3345 Wilshire Boulevard, Suite 1106
Los Angeles, CA 90010

Bibliography: Genetics for High School and College Students

Alliance of Genetic Support Groups
35 Wisconsin Circle, #440
Chevy Chase, MD 20815

Facts About CF

Cystic Fibrosis Foundation
6931 Arlington Road, Suite 200
Bethesda, MD 20814

INDEX

Page numbers in *italics*
refer to illustrations.

Abortion, 99, 100
ADA (adenosine deami-
    nase) deficiency, 101
Adenine (A), 63, 65, 70
Alanine, 67
Alcoholism, 90
Allergies, 57
Ambrose, Christine, 83
Amino acids, 67–68, 73–
    75, 86, 91
Amniocentesis, 96, 98–
    100
Amylase, 68
Animal model, 92
At risk, 78, 88, 97
Avery, O. T., 60

Bases, 63, 65, 70, 85, 86
Becker, Carolyn, *16*
Bennett, Darryl, 95–97
Bennett, Kesha, 95–97
Betathalessemia, 51
Birth defects, 86
Blacks, sickle-cell anemia
    and, 48, 51, 52
Bone marrow transplants,
    101

Cancer, 86, 90, 102–105
Carbon, 75
Carrier, 48
Cell membrane, 22
Cells, 13, 18–19, 22–26
    (*see also* DNA; Genetic
    disorders)
Chargaff, Edwin, 63, 65

Chloride ions, 91
Chorionic villus sampling
  (CVS), 98
Chromosome 4, 82, 85
Chromosome 7, 91
Chromosome 15, 93
Chromosome 21, 26, 98,
  99, 108
Chromosomes, 23–26,
  24, 25, 37, 48, 60, 81,
  98, 107, 108
Circulatory system, 18
Cleft lip and palate, 57
Color blindness, 54
Connective tissue, 18
Crick, Francis, 58, 59, 62,
  63, 65
Cystic fibrosis (CF), 45–
  46, 48, 50, 52, 91, 92,
  101–102
Cytoplasm, 22, 73
Cytosine (C), 63, 65,
  70

Darwin, Charles, 51
Deafness, 92
Deletion, 86
Deoxyribonucleic acid
  (see DNA)
Diabetes, 51, 57, 104
Digestive system, 19
DNA (deoxyribonucleic
  acid), 13–14, 58, 59,
  60–63, 62, 65, 68, 70,
  72, 74–76, 80, 85, 86,
  91, 93, 106, 108–110

Dominant inheritance,
  22, 36–38, 40, 42,
  110
Dopamine, 105
Double helix, 62, 65
Double Helix, The (Wat-
  son), 60
Down's syndrome, 26,
  96–100
Duchenne's muscular dys-
  trophy, 54
Duyao, Mabel, 83

Egg cells, 17, 19, 26, 29,
  34, 40, 53
Embryo, 53, 92
Employers, 88–89, 110
Endoplasmic reticulum,
  69
Enzymes, 67, 74, 101
Ethnic groups, genetic
  disorders and, 51–53
Exons, 91
Eyes, 19, 20

Family trees, 20–22, 26
Fertilization, 19, 26, 34
Fetus, 97
Fibrillin, 93
Franklin, Rosalind, 63, 65

Genes, 13, 19–22, 24–26,
  60, 61 (see also DNA;
  Genetic disorders)
Gene therapy, 101–106,
  109

Genetic counseling, 95–100

Genetic disorders, 14, 17–18, 42, 44

cystic fibrosis (CF), 45–46, 48, 50, 52, 91, 92, 101–102

Huntington's disease (HD), 78, 80–82, 85, 86, 88, 89, 110

Marfan's syndrome, 17–18, 20, 26, 29, 42, 93

prenatal testing and, 93, 96–100

sex-linked inheritance, 48, 53–54, 56

sickle-cell anemia, 48, 49, 50, 52, 85, 96, 97

Tay-Sachs disease, 50–51, 52

Waardenburg's syndrome, 92

Glutamine, 86

G_{M2} ganglioside, 50

Guanine (G), 63, 65, 70

Gusella, James, 82, 83, 85

Hair, 19, 20

Health insurance, 88–89, 110

Heart attacks, 90

Helix, 63, 65

Hemoglobin, 19, 48, 86

Hemophilia, 54, 56

Hereditary Disease Foundation, 80

High blood pressure, 57

Human Genome Project, 106, 108

Huntington's disease (HD), 78, 80–82, 85, 86, 88, 89, 110

HuP2, 92

Hydrogen, 75

Hyman, Flo, 15, 16, 17, 29, 44, 67, 93

Immune system, 101, 103

Inheritance disorders (see Genetic disorders)

Insertion, 86

Insulin, 104

Introns, 91

Jews, Tay-Sachs disease and, 50–52

Jones, Steve, 90–91

Leukemia, 103

Lincoln, Abraham, 18, 93

MacDonald, Marcy, 83

Malaria, 52

Manic-depressive disorders, 90

Marfan's syndrome, 17–18, 20, 26, 29, 42, 93

Mendel, Gregor, 30–37, 32, 40–42, 44, 60, 67, 109
Messenger RNA (*see* mRNA)
Metastasis, 103
Mitochondria, 22, 67
Molecules, 19, 58, 63
mRNA (messenger RNA), 70, 73–75, 74, 85
Mulligan, Richard, 106
Multifactorial disorders, 56–57
Mutation, 85–86, 91

National Institutes of Health, 101
Natural selection, 51
Nature/nurture debate, 90
Negrette, Americo, 81
Nervous system, 18
Nitrogen, 75
Nucleus, 13, 22–23, 69, 72

Organisms, 42
Oxygen, 19, 48, 50, 75

Parkinson's disease, 105
Pax-3, 92
"PEG" treatment, 101
Phenylalanine, 91
Pistil, 34

Placenta, 98
Pollution, 86
Polygenic characteristics, 56
Polypeptides, 76
Prenatal testing, 93, 96–100
Proteins, 67–68, 69, 70, 91

Recessive inheritance, 36–38, 40, 42, 46, 48, 49, 50–51, 110
Red blood cells, 23, 48, 49
Ribonucleic acid (*see* RNA)
Ribosomes, 22, 68, 69, 70, 74, 74, 109
RNA (ribonucleic acid), 72, 75
  mRNA (messenger RNA), 70, 73–75, 74, 85
  tRNA (transfer RNA), 73–75

Schizophrenia, 57
Serine, 67
Sex chromosomes, 24, 53–54
Sex-linked inheritance, 48, 53–54, 56, 110
Sickle-cell anemia, 48, 49, 50, 52, 85, 96, 97
Skeletal system, 18

Smoking, 90
Sperm cells, 17, 19, 26,
  29, 34, 40, 53
Stamens, 34
Structural proteins, 67
Substitution, 85
"Suicide gene," 104

Tay-Sachs disease, 50–51,
  52
Testing (*see* Prenatal test-
  ing)
Threonine, 67
Thymine (T), 63, 65, 70
Tissues, 18
Transfer RNA
  (*see* tRNA)
Trinucleotide repeat, 86
tRNA (transfer RNA),
  73–75

Tumor necrosis factor,
  103

Uracil, 70

Waardenburg's syndrome,
  92
Watson, James, 58, 59,
  60–63, 65
Wexler, Nancy, 77–78,
  79, 80–82, 88–90, 106,
  108, 109
White blood cells, 103
Wilkins, Maurice, 61

X chromosome, 53–54
X-ray diffraction crystallography, 61, 62

Y chromosome, 53, 108